INSIDE THE DIVIDE

INSIDE THE DIVIDE

One City, Two Teams
The Old Firm

Richard Wilson

CANONGATE

Edinburgh · London

Published by Canongate Books in 2012

1

Copyright © Richard Wilson, 2012

The moral right of the author has been asserted

First published in Great Britain in 2012 by Canongate Books Ltd, 14 High Street,
Edinburgh EH1 1TE

www.canongate.tv

British Library Cataloguing-in-Publication Data
A catalogue record for this book is available on
request from the British Library

ISBN 978 1 84767 838 6

Book design by Cluny Sheeler.

Typeset in Minion by Palimpsest Book Production Ltd,
Falkirk, Stirlingshire

Printed and bound in Great Britain by CPI Group (UK) Ltd, Croydon, CR0 4YY

For Pam, who makes anything seem possible and without whom I would be lost; and for Amelia and Christopher, who may never truly know just what they mean to us

CONTENTS

ACKNOWLEDGMENTS

This book began several decades ago, when I took from my father, Jack Wilson, a love for football. Growing up in Glasgow, then becoming by way of one or two detours a sports writer in the city, the Old Firm have seemed ever-present in my life. I share an obsession with these two clubs – Rangers and Celtic – with hundreds of thousands of people, and yet it somehow remains personal. Perhaps the need was always there to address the rivalry, at least as I see it, and so this is an attempt to look at the derby match from the inside, from the perspective of all the different people involved. I chose one Old Firm game at random (the first one that was played after I found a publisher), and happened upon the fixture at Celtic Park on 3 January 2010. This is as comprehensive a study of that game as it could be, but inevitably there were participants who did not wish to contribute.

So the book is an amalgam of original interviews, meticulous research, and some literary licence. The passages in italics that intersperse each chapter are dramatic representations, informed by the people I have spoken to for the book and during more than ten years of covering the Old Firm for various national newspapers. They are an attempt to bring to life what it is like to be in the midst of these games and their aftermath. Throughout the book, where people are quoted directly, the remarks come from interviews or research. Any other quotes are dramatic dialogue, informed but recreated. So much is written and said about the players and managers involved that I wanted to explore the other individuals drawn into the game, but I felt that any Old Firm book still needed to include the experiences of the football men. The purpose is not to present a history of the Old Firm – some unsurpassable books have already been written on this subject – or to glamorise it, but to try to understand it. They are compelling matches, for all their controversies, and I have attempted to capture how they impact on those involved.

During the writing of the book, season 2010–11 reached a crescendo. Seven Old Firm games were played in one season, several red cards were shown, along with too many yellow cards to mention; there were touchline altercations, political ramifications and, worst of all, bullets and parcel bombs sent to the Celtic manager, Neil Lennon. Suddenly, the game seemed belittled by the social and cultural aspects that surround it. This derby match should be celebrated – for its colour, its passion, and its intensity – but there are times when it leaves you cold and forlorn. I hope all of these sentiments are reflected in the book, but also the faith that what makes the game so special will outlive the worst of its excesses.

I am indebted to numerous people and organisations, and if I happen to miss any out, then please accept it as a lapse rather than a slight. In no particular order, I could not have written this book without the following: Carol Patton, Iain Jamieson, Michelle Watt, Jennifer Brophy, Martin Murray, Nigel Tilson, Rob Shorthouse, Wayne Mawson, Darryl Broadfoot, Hugh Dallas, Professor Tom Devine, Michael Grant, Bill Murray, Dave Allan, Marc Chaplain, Caireen Kelly, Jonathan Sim, Alex Henderson, Jamie Watt, Eamonn Hewitt, Dr Michael Sheridan, Gerry McDade, Paul Brennan, David Edgar, Professor Graham Walker, Richard Gordon, Ian Crocker, Professor Steve Bruce, Harald Brattbakk, Darrell King, Donald Cowey and Jonathan Jobson; but also every Old Firm player and manager I have spoken to during my career. It is often a fraught relationship between football and the media, but almost without exception I have learned something from all of you.

I am fortunate to have enjoyed access to an extensive newspaper database, with the most helpful sources of material and insight often being the Scottish press, including the *Herald*, the *Sunday Herald*, the *Scotsman, Scotland on Sunday*, the *Daily Record*, the *Sunday Mail*, the Scottish *Sun*, the Scottish *News of the World*, the Scottish *Daily Express*, the Scottish *Sunday Express*, the Scottish *Daily Mail* and the Scottish *Mail on Sunday*, but other newspapers were also useful. In addition, the following resources were consulted: *Sectarianism in Glasgow* by NFO Social Research; *Challenging Sectarianism in Scotland: The Prism of Racism* by Elinor Kelly, as well as several books, including: *The Old Firm* and *Bhoys, Bears and Bigotry* by Bill Murray; *Voices of the Old Firm* by Stephen Walsh; *Sectarianism in Scotland* by Steve Bruce; *Butcher: My Autobiography* by Terry Butcher; *Hail Cesar: The Autobiography* by Billy McNeill; *John Greig: My Story*; *Shooting Star: The Colin Stein Story*; *Gazza: My Story* by Paul Gascoigne; *Graeme Souness: A Manager's Diary*; and *The Management* by Michael Grant and Rob Robertson. Several radio and television programmes were also helpful, including *Alternative Histories of the Old Firm* and *Managing the Old Firm* on BBC Radio Scotland, and Neil Lennon's interview on RTE's *Saturday Night With Miriam*.

I should mention that for all things Rangers I continue to cherish the impassioned conversations of Craig Wilson, Euan Dow and Chris Cole, with the occasional, but always distinctive, input of Neil Anderson. For Celtic, there are few more informed, or worthwhile, opinions than those of Andrew H. Smith and Hugh MacDonald. All are friends, but I value our football chats, too. This book would not exist without the support and belief of David Luxton, my agent, who is never short of encouragement or, indeed, patience. The same applies to all at Canongate, for whom it has been a pleasure and an honour to write. Dan Franklin was the first person to share my own level of enthusiasm for the idea, then Nick Davies was a source of endless improvements. Norah Perkins has always been a beacon of positivity, while Seán Costello's editing was meticulous, insightful and helpful. All played a part in transforming the book from a vague idea and some rough writing, but the same should be said for Neil White, a friend and colleague whose initial eagerness provided the impetus to take the book on, but also provided some much-needed cheer at a difficult time.

Finally, I would like to take the opportunity to say thanks to my father, for many things that do not need to be said, but also for driving me to football training and matches several times a week when I was a boy, and for standing on the touchline of some run-down park, in all extremes of weather, to watch me. You never knew how reassuring that was. Sometime very early on, the game became our connection, which is why it means so much to me now. I also owe more than gratitude to my wife, Pam, and my two children, Amelia and Christopher. You put up with the unsociable hours, the holidays spent immersed in researching and writing, the stress of trying to meet the deadlines, but never without a word of support or love. I couldn't have felt alone, because you continue to be my greatest inspiration, but I often felt selfish. I hope that in some small way, the book was worth it. Your opinion is, always, the only one that matters. Thank you, for everything.

PROLOGUE

The day starts early, in thousands of homes in cities, villages and towns across Scotland and beyond. It is dark outside, and the freezing cold air is cruelly sharp and clear. Time is slipping away, and the sense is of a need to be somewhere else, to be on the move; the first of the ferries and the buses will leave soon, they will not hold back for stragglers. On the way out of the front door, a final check: wallet, keys, phone, ticket. Ticket, that is essential. One last look: Celtic v. Rangers, Celtic Park, 3 January 2010.

Across Scotland, the Republic of Ireland, Northern Ireland and England, the game is already a presence, while around the globe, plans are being finalised for watching live television coverage; the vast Scottish and Irish diaspora grasping on to a last remnant of their past. No other game in world football can claim the same reach into the hearts and psychology of so many people, touching something beyond a mere appreciation of football and what the outcome of a single match might mean. Hundreds of thousands of supporters will follow the game's every nuance, drawn together by its intrigues. Celtic are seven points behind Rangers in the Scottish Premier League, having lost the first Old Firm match of the season, at Ibrox, 2–1. There is, too, a sharper edge, with it being only the second Ne'er Day game in ten years. The traditional fixture, once always played on New Year's Day, had been moved to later in the season because old, deep-seated antagonisms and the diminished restraints of the festive period had combined into something unmanageable, a recklessness. Supporters drank heavily, released by the freedom of days off work, and the occasion became too fraught to contain because of the volatile mix of alcohol and hostility. So the fixture on this day carries with it a sense of anxious anticipation.

On separate early-morning ferries from Northern Ireland, arranged especially for the match, rival supporters are carried across to Scotland. The boats are full, and a reputation for boorish, occasionally aggressive behaviour on these trips lingers. There is a dark sense of humour among the travellers, as they eat cooked breakfasts and flick through the newspapers, discussing the game: who will play, who should play, who they cherish, who they despise; what the outcome will mean, why their team has to win, and why they hate the other side so much. There is a hardness to so many of them, a rough, uncompromising nature, that they seem withdrawn, sullen even. When the boat catches a swell and lurches momentarily, they don't flinch. When the ferry lands, and a breeze whips scraps of rubbish around the dock, they pull their jackets tight to them and squint as they disembark, while security guards and police watch them from a distance.

The journey is symbolic, in that it represents the two great flows of migration from Ireland that have shaped the Old Firm rivalry. Rangers were formed in 1872 by a group of young men – Moses and Peter McNeill, two brothers, and Peter Campbell and William McBeath – keen to involve themselves in a sport whose popularity was growing briskly, but with no religious influence. It was 1888 before Celtic were established, by Brother Walfrid, a Marist, to raise money for soup kitchens that would look after members of the Catholic population while keeping them within the faith by providing an alternative to those run by Protestants. A religious divide existed, in the sense that Rangers, like most other Scottish clubs, were essentially a Protestant organisation (as it was the country's dominant religion), and Celtic were mostly followed by and run for Catholics, a small but growing part of the population as the prospect of employment in heavy industry brought workers across the Irish Sea.

By the time of the next significant wave of immigrants from Ireland, in the early twentieth century, Celtic had supplanted Hibernian, the Edinburgh team, as the pre-eminent club of the Catholic population, an ethnic minority that faced persecution culturally and in the workplace by the mainly Protestant society. Rangers, due to the club's substantial following, great success and presence in Glasgow, was the club of the Protestant majority. (Even though Rangers had not been formed with any religious affiliation, an unwritten policy was eventually established, and mostly maintained until the 1990s, of preferring to sign non-Catholics.) The Irish workers, of both religions, brought with them a more acute, more belligerent hatred and distrust of each other, so that the rivalry between the two teams, which had always been pronounced, even encouraged – the term, the Old Firm, is thought to have been coined by a newspaper to reflect the fact that the clubs recognised the economic value of the competition between them – became darker, more malign. The Catholic population were downtrodden, the Protestants felt threatened, and a kind of barrier was erected, with a sense of victimisation on one side, and a pious defensiveness on the other.

By the end of the nineteenth century, Old Firm games were attracting crowds of 50,000 people, but also the kind of heightened emotions and aggression that would spill over into violence. A New Year's Day game at Celtic Park in 1898 was stopped with the scoreline at 1–1 because fans invaded the pitch, mostly infuriated at refereeing decisions. In 1909, the two sides contested the Scottish Cup final, with a 1–1 draw leading to a replay. When this, too, ended in a draw, supporters were so disgruntled at the prospect of paying to attend another fixture that they rioted, causing hundreds of pounds' worth of damage. Small fires were started, and the fire-fighters who attended to them were attacked. More than a hundred people were injured, and as a consequence of the rioting, the Scottish Cup was withheld that season. Even through the war years, when football became a small but welcome distraction, Old Firm games still tended to suffer intermittent moments of crowd trouble, while attracting large attendances. This combination, of the tense rivalry and the sheer scale of the following of the two clubs, began to set the fixture apart from the rest of Scottish football in its intensity and its significance. Harland and Wolff, the Belfast shipbuilders, opened a yard on the River Clyde in 1912, bringing with them workers from Northern Ireland and some hardened prejudices (they were widely believed to have favoured Protestant employees over Catholics) that further influenced the Old Firm rivalry.

Supporters travel to Celtic Park on this January morning from all across Scotland, but predominantly from west and central areas. Buses – some of them little more than twelve-seaters, rusty and blanched with age, others full-sized coaches – wait at designated collection points, often pub car parks, even though on a Sunday morning the premises are closed. As the supporters wait to board, standing in close groups and moving in that anxious, distracted way, their breath immediately clouds, as if in grievance at the chill air. Scarves are wrapped tightly round their necks, and cigarette ends glow a fading orange in the dim light. Once on the bus – which has a picture of the pope wearing a Celtic top taped to the back window – the mood lightens. Flags are draped across the back windows, songs are sung, drink (although not allowed by the police) is discreetly consumed, and an air of excited detachment fills the journey. Chants begin among the Celtic fans:

> Oh Willie Maley was his name,
> He brought some great names to the game,
> When he was the boss at Celtic Park.

Taught them how to play football
He made the greatest of them all,
Gallagher and Quinn have left their mark.
And they gave us James McGrory and Paul McStay,
They gave us Johnstone, Tully, Murdoch, Auld and Hay,
And most of the football greats,
Have passed through Parkhead's gates,
All to play football the Glasgow Celtic way

And among the Rangers fans:

For the cry was No Surrender,
Surrender or you'll die (die! die!)
With heart and hand and sword and shield,
We'll guard old Derry's walls.

King James and all his rebel scum,
Came up to Bishop's Gate,
With heart and hand and sword and shield,
We forced them to retreat.

Altogether now!
The cry was No Surrender
Surrender or you'll die (die! die!)

A camaraderie asserts itself among the different groups, a shared sense of identity. 'We'll murder that mob today,' a voice says. 'Ah bloody hope so,' says another, quietly.

The Old Firm are unique, in the sense that no other rivalry in world football is primarily predicated along religious lines. In England, it is not uncommon for members of the same family to support Liverpool or Everton, and travel to matches between the two sides together. The North London derby between Arsenal and Tottenham Hotspur is capable of vindictiveness – standing in amongst the home fans behind one of the goals at Highbury several years ago, near to where the Tottenham supporters were housed, it was possible to hear a sustained and spreading hissing sound. It was a section of the Arsenal crowd replicating the noise of the gas chambers, since Tottenham's following has historically included a large number of Jewish supporters. But as with the Manchester derby, which can also be spiteful – City fans, for instance, sing disparagingly about the 1958 Munich disaster, when members of the famous Busby Babes Manchester United team died in a plane crash – the rivalry does not match the intensity of Celtic v. Rangers, since the two Manchester clubs have not been regularly vying with each other for honours. English football considers Liverpool v. Manchester United a derby match, as the clubs have competed with each other for dominance through the years, but that fixture lacks the urgency and significance of a game between two sides from the same city. With English teams only playing each other twice a season, and there being a number of high-profile, pressurised fixtures on top of the entrenched rivalries – such as Chelsea v. Arsenal or Arsenal v. Manchester United – no single match is as charged as the Old Firm encounter.

In Europe, Real Madrid v. Barcelona is known as *El Clásico*, or the derby of Spain, since the two sides represent their regions – Castile and Catalonia – but also the political dominance of Madrid, and Catalan independence. They are also the two largest and most successful clubs in Spain, often battle with each other for the La Liga title, and stand for something more in their communities than merely a football team. Barcelona, in particular, were a source of Catalan defiance during Franco's reign, when the dictator attempted to suppress the various regional identities in Spain and emphasise the status of Madrid as the nation's seat of power. In terms of political and social significance, *El Clásico* comes closest to the Old Firm game, but does not carry with it the same depth of history or, again, the immediacy of the two communities living together in the same city.

In Italy, Roma v. Lazio is a local derby with political currency – the mostly left-wing Roma fans and the right-wing Lazio supporters – while the biggest derby match in South America is Boca Juniors v. River Plate, and although both teams originate from the same poor area of Buenos Aries, River moved to a different, more affluent part of the city and came to be known as *Los Millonarios*, representing a wealthier tier of the population. Egyptian football is dominated by two Cairo clubs – Al-Ahly and Zamalek – who are also recognised as the most successful teams in Africa and whose fans will often resort to violence after games. Istanbul is, like Glasgow, a city that considers football part of its heritage and its identity, so that the game causes a fervour among supporters. Matches between Galatasaray and Fenerbahce, two of the country's most prominent clubs, are fraught and fan violence is not uncommon, with Galatasaray based on the European side of the Bosphorus and said to represent the aristocratic class, while Fenerbahce are on the Asian side and said to be the club of the working-class people. The two teams are widely supported throughout Turkey, but the presence of a third local side – Besiktas – adds another layer of rivalry and so diminishes something of the intensity of the Kitalar-Arasi Derbi (or Intercontinental Derby). Yet while all these games evoke passion and anger, loyalty and fanaticism, identity and a sense of belonging, it is the Old Firm derby that is unique in representing a clash of religions, making the political and cultural aspects of the rivalry more fraught and far-reaching.

Celtic v. Rangers still, 122 years after the clubs' first match, represents Catholic v. Protestant. In Glasgow, where the grime of heavy industry still clings to every surface, all the edges – of its buildings, its people, its institutions, its outlook, its humour – are hard and razor-edged. It is a fractured place. There is a bleakness to areas of the city, a despairing air caused by poverty, drug use, alcoholism, crime: the symptoms of hopelessness; but also neighbouring districts of wealth, community, middle-class entitlement. If there is a common trait, it is the dry, black wit that shapes the opportunism of the addict and the criminal as much as the lawyer and the doctor. Even the River Clyde, which runs along the edge of the city centre in a deep, slow weave, often looks grey and surly, as if reflecting still the great shipbuilding clamour of the past.

A working-class city, frank and unabashed in its views, Glasgow's self-esteem came to rely upon football. The three largest stadiums in the world were once here, and Ibrox, Celtic Park and Hampden are still among the biggest grounds in Britain. Football once provided Glaswegians, and Scots in general, with another outlet for their sense of superiority, an ingrained haughtiness that delighted in the wry but truculent eminence of the likes of Jim Baxter, Dennis Law, Billy Bremner and Jimmy Johnstone. There are fewer justifications now for that conceit, when greatness has seeped from the bloodline of Scottish footballers, but the game itself retains its power, the notion that the country is still relevant outwith its borders, that it remains a place – in its devotion to and its influence on football – to be reckoned with. There was a time, from the mid-1960s to the mid-1970s, when Celtic and Rangers were among the most admired teams in Europe. Celtic, under the shrewd management of Jock Stein – one of Scottish football's iconic figures – became the first British side to win the European Cup when they defeated Internazionale in Lisbon in 1967, while in the same year Rangers lost in the European Cup-Winners' Cup final to Bayern Munich. Scottish football, and the Old Firm in particular, was able to savour its moments of glory. Celtic reached the European Cup final again in 1970, only to lose to Feyenoord, while Rangers won the European Cup-Winners' Cup in 1973, the team guided to its triumph by Willie Waddell. These were the heady days of Celtic and Rangers, when players like Jimmy Johnstone and Billy McNeill, and John Greig and Jim Baxter, were world-class footballers, but also typically Scottish in their brashness.

The Old Firm game is not so much a part of Glasgow as among its defining characteristics, a last connection with the people and the industry that once brought the city such prominence in the Empire. Heavy manufacturing has dwindled, to be replaced by call centres and the service economy, while the universities are now no more significant cradles for intellect, culture and art than those in other cities across the UK. Instead, Glasgow is a place distinguished by its areas of poverty, low life expectancy, drug and alcohol dependency as much as its grand history and sense of aggressive defiance; it has become a city of contradictions, where deprivation and privilege co-exist. Football remains central to all its communities, like a defining birthright. But then, absurdity resides even in the darkest corners of Glasgow life; it is often said that on the afternoon in October 1971 when Celtic lost the League Cup final to Partick Thistle at Hampden, hundreds of Rangers supporters left Ibrox early, where their team was playing in the league, to make the short journey to the national stadium and join in the humiliation of their old rivals. More recently, when Celtic supporters were anticipating playing in the Uefa Cup final against Porto in Spain in 2003, they threw beach balls onto the pitch at Ibrox during an Old Firm game and chanted: 'You'll be watching *The Bill* while we're in Seville'.

Every Old Firm game is informed by this history, as Glasgow's political, cultural and religious background has shaped a rivalry so fierce, so entrenched, so distinct, that the populace can be split into two along this single line of division. There are Rangers areas of the city and Celtic areas; Rangers pubs and Celtic pubs; non-denominational schools and Catholic schools. Even though the two religious communities have never been more assimilated, Scotland is the only country in the world to have an anti-sectarian law, which has arisen in response to the crimes of violence and abuse that gather around Old Firm games, and so pits Catholic against Protestant in the context of a heated football contest. The Old Firm rivalry is still something intense, something grimly fascinating; it is capable of inspiring greatness in those players who can rise to the pressure and perform. Yet it also generates a sense of outrage among the supporters as they respond to each other, and the wider Scottish community, which reacts to the fierceness of the games with disdain while treating it as a guilty pleasure; the nation abhors the violence that the Old Firm matches can incite, but is at the same time enthralled by them.

At train stations on this Sunday morning, fans mingle in small groups, or travel alone on their way to meet friends. Often, scarves are stuffed out of view, so that trouble is avoided, at least when supporters are outwith the protection of a crowd. Many are preoccupied, a little subdued by the time of day and a sense of vague disquiet. On match days, the Glasgow subway is thronged with people, and the train drivers can hear the waiting supporters even before their train emerges from the dank blackness of the tunnels. As it approaches the circle of light where the platform begins, the only thought in the driver's mind is that a fan, drunk and heedless, might tumble onto the track. Rangers supporters use the subway to travel to Ibrox for home games, but fans also use it to head for Buchanan Street or St Enoch in the city centre, from where they can walk to Celtic Park, or Partick, where they can take an overground train out to the east end. Often, when there is standing room only on the subway carriages and they are noticeably heavy to the drivers, the Rangers supporters have been known to jump up and down in unison and sing, 'Bouncy Bouncy, Bouncy Bouncy, Ra, Ra, Ra', causing the carriages to jolt and momentarily leave the tracks. Occasionally, amid the boisterousness, drivers are forced to stop the train and warn the fans that it might crash.

Cars and buses park in the streets around Celtic Park, which sits off the side of London Road. As people spill out of the vehicles, they seem briefly disorientated in the stark winter sunlight. The stadium rises above its surroundings of small, box houses and nondescript warehouses, its roof jutting into the pale blue sky. The pace quickens, and the supporters start to crane their necks, trying to see the body of the stadium. Piles of frozen, dirty snow have been pushed to the edge of the pavement, but it is still icy underfoot. Nobody speaks, unless in low, gruff voices, and a young boy grasps his father's hand tightly. They cross a side street and, to their left, police officers are gathering, up by the side of a small, flat building, wearing bright yellow jackets and impassive expressions. A voice suddenly rises from further ahead, a rasping Irish accent. 'There's the bus, there they are. Dirty Orange bastards.' The coach carrying the Rangers team to Celtic Park drives by, flanked by police motorcycles. 'I hope they've paid their fare,' shouts another voice. Shadowed faces can be seen behind the darkened glass, watching. More voices rise now, loud, fierce, defiant. 'Cel-tic. Cel-tic. Cel-tic.'

The father and son pass a man selling scarves and glittering gold badges that are pinned to a blackboard. '*Not the View*, latest issue,' another man shouts, brandishing the Celtic fanzine. Then a small coach abruptly pulls up at the side of the road, white with blue lettering – Ulsterbus – and a handful of people tumble out, men and women in Celtic jerseys, gingerly picking their way along the edges of the pavement, where flattened, dirty snow is still smeared, but buoyant and cheerful to have finished their journey. 'We're here to see the Holy Goalie,' one of them says, using the nickname for Artur Boruc, Celtic's Polish goalkeeper.

From the edge of the car park that lies in front of Celtic Park, the stadium rises into view again, behind a consternation of movement – the jerking, unsteady progress of parking cars and people – and a grumbling noise; there is an air of deep apprehension, something potent but also fragile among the growing crowds of people. The car park is full, and people make their way through the lines of vehicles with grave concentration. Stewards form a line from the reception doors, down the red brick steps to the Rangers coach, and as the players disembark, one by one and looking either pensive or self-absorbed, they are clattered with abuse. It is ritualistic, as though the fans are compelled to join in and the players expect to endure it, although some provoke a greater stir than others, particularly Nacho Novo, who chose Rangers over Celtic when moving from Dundee in 2004. 'Nacho Novo, fuckin' homo', someone shouts. Police horses look on, drawing shallow breaths. The crowd of Celtic supporters (the away fans are restricted to a small area round the other side of the ground, where they are hemmed in by stewards and police) mingle in the car park and the concourses that surround the stadium. Some clutch plastic carrier bags of merchandise bought from the club superstore next to Celtic Park, others draw heavily on cigarettes – last, agitated gasps – as if breathing in their sense of apprehension. At this moment, in the closeness to the game, the occasion is not about winning, but about not losing to them, the rivals.

For Rangers, seven points ahead in the league and already seeming dominant in this campaign, a win would strengthen their command and cast further doubt on their opponents; for Celtic, a victory would draw the Ibrox side back within reach and renew both the team's determination and the conviction of Tony Mowbray's management. He is under scrutiny, for his tactics, his demeanour, his lack of leadership; all of which stands in contrast to the time-served authority of Walter Smith, his Rangers counterpart, who has made a career of seeing off Celtic managers and whose Old Firm record is imposing. Smith, too, has retained the team's competitiveness despite financial cutbacks that have seen every player effectively put up for sale and the manager unable to sign any replacements while Lloyds Bank begin to recoup the massive debt run up by the owner, Sir David Murray. So for Celtic, this is a time when their great rivals are teetering on the edge of calamity, but they have been too indecisive to push them over the edge.

All of these tensions gather around the game, and are shaped by the historical baggage: the religious, social and political complexities. All the influences are present at Celtic Park: in the mood of the supporters, in their facial expressions, in the minds of the players and the coaching staff, the referee, the police, the stewards, even in the rest of the city; all are aware of a sense of anticipation.

CHAPTER 1
KICK-OFF

Look straight ahead, don't catch anybody's eye. Fuck's sake, this is it. Stretch, bounce. Did I tie my laces tight enough? Don't smile, don't look nervous; don't give them anythin'. We cannae lose, not this game. Look at them, what are they thinking? Just concentrate, remember whit you've been told and win the first tackle, win it hard, no prisoners, no' the day. We need to win this game. And be calm, don't be gettin' caught up in anything. That ref'll be all over us, he gives nothin' away. And watch for him comin' infield, remember that, when he lines up to shoot; you've got to close him down. If he gets a clean shot away in this game, the gaffer will be fuckin' raging. Come on, you've got to be up for this today, in their faces, right-a-fuckin' way. And for Christ's sake don't be caught ball-watching, because he's good in the air, and he'll fuckin' have you.

Jesus, when's this fuckin' referee leading us out. Come on. Don't be intimidated, play your game. That's why you're in the team, because you're good enough. You can do it out there. Keep your cool, don't get dragged into anything. Be smart. And don't do anything stupid. The gaffer said to keep it simple, and he means it. No fancy shit today. Do your job. That's all you need to do out there. Fuck's sake, bloody palms are sweating and everything. Come on.

Right, out the tunnel now. Here we go. Into that fuckin' noise. Jesus. Jesus. Look at them all, fuckin' hell. That noise. Fuck me. Right, routine. Run and stretch. Run and stretch. Got to limber up. Just be *normal, do the usual stuff. Look at those fans, they're nuts. Maybe a wee scowl for them, just so they know I'm up for this, and they won't get to me. 'Right, here we go lads, this is it. Come on, we're up for this. Let's fuckin' do it. First ball. First tackle. Make it count.' Hurry up, ref, let's get it started. Come on.*

Right we're in it. Nothing else matters but now. Where's the ball? I need that first touch. Wait for the first challenge, it's coming, it'll be a sore one. Take it. Don't show any sign of weakness. Get back up. 'Ref, keep an eye on that, will you? Fuck's sake. C'mon.' He's worried about me, that tackle was desperate, I've got his number. I need to make my mark, show I'm up for this. I'll not be pushed around; this is my game. Right, come on, let's get into this. Who's got the ball? Who's behind me? For fuck's sake, keep the ball, pass the fucking thing, keep it simple. It's not the time for that kind of shit. Close him down. Chase. I need to get involved. Watch him, he's your man, stay on him, stay on him. He's yours. We can't lose, not this game.

Players who have experienced other renowned derby matches, like Barcelona v. Real Madrid, AC Milan v. Internazionale, or Everton v. Liverpool find a greater intensity in the Old Firm fixture, something frenzied and urgent. It is the most significant game, in terms of rivalry, in terms of the league, in terms of its meaning outwith football, that the players will ever encounter, but it is also endless. The two sides meet four times in the league, so the next meeting is never more than three months away, while the build-up and the aftermath make the games more exhausting and collapse the space between them. The games always seem pivotal to the title race (it was 1985 when a club outwith the Old Firm last won the Championship). They are always in the minds of supporters, who feel compelled to tell players of their duty, their obligation to this huge following that they represent.

Foreign players who move to Celtic or Rangers find themselves thrust into the midst of this impassioned throng, and coming to terms with it either emboldens or diminishes them. When players sign for either of the two clubs, they are immediately confronted with the Old Firm game; journalists ask about it straight away – 'What do you know?', 'What have you been told?' – so that it becomes the fixture they are first aware of. Then teammates tell them that beating the other side is all that matters, and supporters say the same in every encounter: 'Just make sure you beat that lot, big man.' The game seems to take on an identity of its own, even before the depth of the religious rivalry is revealed. Many foreign players understand that an Old Firm match represents Protestant v. Catholic, but not the animosity that it generates. Many come from countries where religion remains more influential and routine, such as Italy, Spain and Algeria, and few are prepared for the antagonism that confronts them in Glasgow.

'The game is famous wherever you go in the world. People know about the rivalry,' said Brian Laudrup towards the end of his Rangers career. 'It's recognised everywhere. When I joined up with Denmark soon after joining Rangers, Peter Schmeichel took me aside and said: "I thought the pace of the game in England was quick – but we've got nothing on that [Old Firm game]". He reckoned even a Manchester United–Liverpool match couldn't compare and admitted he'd love to sample that kind of atmosphere. Basile Boli was another player who rated this fixture as highly as anything he'd witnessed. He stunned me once by saying one of our Old Firm clashes had been screened live in France and was voted the best game seen in France that year. I've played in front of 80,000 during an AC Milan–Inter Milan derby and the football has been exceptional. But nowhere beats this game for passion and commitment – on and off the pitch. My brother Michael has also played in massive games in Italy and few matches can compare with the Barcelona–Real Madrid clash he's starred in. But even he admits his one regret is he never managed to experience an Old Firm game – it's the only thing he's envious about. If I learned one thing it's to avoid thinking about Old Firm games beforehand. Inexperienced players can let it eat away at them for weeks – they end up draining themselves of all their energy.'

Gary Lineker played in the North London derby between Arsenal and Tottenham, the Liverpool derby and the Barcelona v. Real Madrid fixture, and although he never featured in an Old Firm game, he attended several of them, which he later wrote about in his newspaper column. 'I can testify that there is nothing to compare with them in terms of their intensity and ferocity, not to mention the sheer noise,' Lineker said. 'And I thought North London derbies were fairly nasty. My view of the Celtic–Rangers games was from a position between both sets of supporters, many of whom were more interested in displaying their hostility towards one another than watching the game. It was the look of hatred on some faces which I will never forget. I found it quite disturbing. The Merseyside derby is a far cry from that. I remember travelling on the Everton team bus to the 1986 FA Cup final against Liverpool and seeing a father in a blue scarf carrying a son in a red one. It may not have been typical, but rivalries within the same family are not uncommon in Liverpool, which probably makes that derby unique. The Barca–Madrid derby is also exceptional inasmuch as the rivalry between fans does not manifest itself at the games since hardly any visiting supporters attend them. There are few things in football quite as bizarre as the hush which descends on a crowd of 120,000 following a goal by the visitors.'

Old Firm players spend less time at supporters' functions than in previous years, but interaction with the fans is a way of life in Glasgow, because even for those living in the suburbs, everything gravitates to, and revolves around, the city centre. Players and fans mingle – in bars, restaurants, clubs, even on golf courses and in high-end shops – while the Scots in the dressing room or the backroom staff make sure that newcomers, particularly foreigners, know what the supporters will expect and how they will express their views. Footballers are no different from the rest of society in that religion is less of a defining issue in their identity, and in many ways the macho atmosphere of the football dressing room offers little scope for the personal expression of a player's faith. As professionals, they are often conditioned to their surroundings, bringing with them a sense of self-preservation, and treating their time at a club as an assignment. 'If you're a Catholic and you play for Rangers, then you're a Protestant,' said Fernando Ricksen, the Dutchman who played for Rangers. 'If you can't handle that, if you're really a Catholic and you feel too much about it, you don't come to Rangers. You stay away. You'd better go to the other side [Celtic] or there will be a lot of problems for you.'

It is this sense of the way that the two clubs exist in absolute opposition to each other that intensifies the Old Firm derby match. Jimmy Nicholl, who played for Manchester United, Rangers and Northern Ireland, once characterised the manic nature of the fixture by recalling a standing ovation he received for winning a throw-in. Ray Wilkins, the former England international, remembered being told to 'take his football head off' for the game, and not even think about trying to play any slow, thoughtful passes.

'My plan was always to try and set the tone in an Old Firm game, you need to let the other side know what you're all about early on,' said Barry Ferguson of his approach to the fixture. 'Whether it's an early shot on goal, a good attacking move or even a crunching tackle, you need to stamp authority on the game. "We are here, we are right up for this, let's be having it." The mental side of an Old Firm game is crucial. You need to try and find any kind of edge. Who has the hunger; who wants it most; who is up for it? You could look around the pitch early on in an Old Firm game and see who was up for it, and who wasn't.'

In playing the game, when it feels as though so much is at stake and the very atmosphere itself is volatile and unnerving, the challenge is often just to remain calm. Ricksen was substituted twenty-two minutes into his Old Firm derby at Celtic Park (which the home side eventually won 6–2) after being terrorised by Bobby Petta, the Dutch left winger. Ricksen later admitted that he had not been prepared for the intensity of the occasion, and teammates spoke of him sitting in the dressing room afterwards looking ashen-faced. It is a fixture in which the crowd, and the players, seem forever on the verge of fury. 'These particular ninety minutes have a habit of throwing up the unexpected – like the day Stefan Klos and I squared up to each other,' recalled Paul Lambert, the Scotland international midfielder, of his experiences playing for Celtic. 'I mean we are good friends from our time at [Borussia] Dortmund together. There was a penalty claim for Celtic and Stefan wasn't for giving us the ball, so we had a wee go and squared up to each other. It's crazy, absolutely stupid behaving like that, but in these games you just get caught up in it.'

It is fear that drives performances in an Old Firm game: the terror of losing, of making a critical mistake, of becoming a scapegoat. Win this match and for a time everything will be calm and untroubled, but lose it and it feels like an act of betrayal. Rangers and Celtic players are surrounded by the communities that look to the two clubs for their sense of identity. The population of Greater Glasgow (the city and its immediate surroundings) is almost 1.8m people, yet the 60,000-seat Celtic Park, and 51,000-seat Ibrox Stadium can be full for even the most mundane of fixtures, with support for the two clubs spreading beyond into the west of Scotland and even out across the rest of the country. So much is bound up in the notion of being

a Celtic or Rangers supporter that it becomes a form of self-defini-
tion: you are one or the other, with us or against us. Old Firm players
feel a responsibility that is informed by their team's vast communities and their values, their obligations, their prejudices, so that the
derby match becomes a test of them as footballers, but also as individuals; they feel duty bound to defeat the other side, and not let
the supporters down.

Glasgow is such a small, self-contained city that there is no respite.
In the affluent suburbs where players tend to live, there is no seclu-
sion and they are surrounded by as many Old Firm fans as they are
when they head into the city centre for a night out. The sense is of
being constantly enclosed, a suffocating feeling that is exacerbated
by the insatiable media attention. For the Scottish players who have
grown up immersed in the rivalry, there is an instinctive understanding of how the antagonisms between the two sets of supporters
are expressed, but it is also personalised by the friends and family
members who are part of these communities. In some ways, it feels
more intimate and more vital because of that, particularly if they
grew up supporting one side or the other themselves. Then, the
tension before Old Firm games can feel even more febrile.

Strong characters thrive on the pressure. Glasgow is an aggressive
place, hard and spiky, with an attitude of feisty self-assurance, but
also a contempt for meekness; people have either grown up in hard,
often violent surroundings that have brutalised their spirit, or they
are aware of this harsh environment because it exists next to them.
And everything seems to revolve around the fortunes of the city's
two major football teams. 'You wake up in the morning and you
think about Celtic, you go training and you think about Celtic, you
pick up a paper and you read about Celtic, you walk down the street
and people with Celtic tops are calling out and you think about
Celtic, and then you go home to sleep and you dream about Celtic,
before you wake up and start all over again, thinking always about

Celtic,' said Neil Lennon at the end of his playing career at the club. 'You think about the game coming up, and every game is a big game, every game is a "must-win" for Celtic. I have had that pressure for nearly seven years and I'll tell you, I've loved it all. It has been a really intense time in my life and it has been truly fulfilling and rewarding.'

Peter Grant played in fifty Old Firm games for Celtic, and when the team lost 5–1 to Rangers at Ibrox in 1988, he was so ashamed that he did not leave his house for four days except to go to training and, once, to visit the chapel. 'Celtic consumed me as a player. I loved being part of Celtic, but whether I enjoyed it is a different question,' he later reflected on his fifteen years at Parkhead. 'The intensity of this club, going straight from being a fan to playing for Celtic, was huge. Both my grandfathers ran Celtic supporters' buses and the club was all I knew.'

To players who have grown up supporting either of the two sides, the matches are more personal; they are experienced both as a fan and as a participant. Ally McCoist once remarked that there were some Old Firm games that made him feel like lying down in a darkened room afterwards, and the sense is always of trying to survive them. A win is not so much enjoyed as treated as a source of relief, while a defeat becomes a burden. Billy Dodds, the former Rangers striker, played at Celtic Park when the visitors lost 6–2, and remembered the journey back to Ibrox as being desolate. 'The silence on the bus was deafening,' he later revealed. 'No one dared to speak. Suddenly, I looked up and glanced out of the window. Hundreds of heartbroken Rangers fans were lining the streets. Each one had his arms wide open as if to ask, "What the fuck happened, lads?" I'd never been so embarrassed in all my life. I couldn't shake the feeling we'd let them all down. That feeling stayed with me for weeks. The Old Firm match gets inside your head, your heart, and doesn't let go.'

*There's no time to breathe here, it just doesn't stop. Christ, I wish
somebody would go down injured or something, just to get a
minute's peace. I need a drink of water, my mouth is dry. Where's
the ball? Where's that guy? And what's he shouting? I can't hear
a bloody word he's saying. I need to get into this match, show
what I can do, show that I can play in these games. Christ, it's
frantic. 'Feet, feet, play it to feet. For fuck's sake, how am I
supposed to chase that down? Hey, play it to my fucking feet will
you?' Fucking idiot. I need a chance, just one, I'll get at this
defender, either skin him or he'll bring me down. C'mon, get me
on the ball, get it over this way. I fucking hate them and their
fans, they give out nothing but abuse. Bastards. I'll show them.
Right, past him, and . . . nobody there. Not one fucker in the
right place in the box. That was a great ball in, what chance do
you have? Next time.*

On 12 May 1989, Maurice Johnston posed for pictures at Parkhead,
clutching a green-and-white hooped jersey and standing next to Billy
McNeill, the Celtic manager. 'I didn't want to leave Celtic [in 1987,
when he joined Nantes], and I don't intend to now', Johnston said.
'There was some rubbish about me wanting to join Manchester
United, but it never entered my head to play for any other club. In
fact, there is no other British club I could play for apart from Celtic.'
At twenty-six, and approaching the peak of his career, the striker
wanted to return to Celtic Park, where he had first established himself
as a quick-witted, streetwise goal-scorer, and something of a playboy.
With his cocksure, insouciant attitude and his dyed blond hair, Johnston was a charismatic footballer but also an arch finisher. In France,
his ability had been refined (he was always a hard trainer, which made
up for his fondness for enjoying the nightlife), so that his movement

and appreciation of the geometry of the game were sharpened. A deal was agreed between Johnston and the club, with the player signing paperwork and Celtic making a £400,000 down-payment on a reported £1.2m transfer fee (Johnston also secretly joined the Celtic players on the team bus to a game at St Mirren before the season ended). Then on 10 July 1989, Johnston signed for Rangers.

The move was typical of Graeme Souness, the Ibrox manager: brash, confrontational, audacious and shrewd. From the moment he arrived at the club in the summer of 1986, Souness wanted to end the unofficial policy of not signing Catholics on a moral level – his wife and children were Catholic – but also because it seemed to him absurd that such an outdated practice could be allowed to hold the team back. To him, it was a measure of the club's attitude and stature, and so a reflection of his management, that they sought to sign the very best players, however much they cost, and regardless of their background. It was an attitude he shared with David Murray, the Edinburgh businessman who bought Rangers in 1988, having been made aware of the club's availability by his friend, Souness. As with the majority of his decisions at Ibrox, the Rangers manager wanted to be bold, to make a statement of his intent, but also of his own sophistication and single-mindedness. He was desperate for Terry Butcher, the first of his keynote signings, to turn out to be Catholic, but instead had to rely on his status as England captain to make an impact on Scottish football and beyond. Souness later sounded out players like Ian Rush, John Sheridan, John Collins and Ray Houghton about becoming a high-profile Catholic signing at Ibrox, to no avail, with some unwilling to provoke the ire of the Catholic community in Glasgow by joining Rangers. Then he learned of Johnston's desire to return to Scotland, and sought out the striker's agent, Bill McMurdo.

There remain some ambiguities about how the move unfolded, but Celtic were adamant that Johnston was effectively their player (a stance later supported by Fifa), even though he backed out of the agreement. Once Celtic began to realise that the player wasn't committed to the original transfer, McNeill confronted him while he was staying at the Marine Hotel in Troon with the Scotland squad. Andy Roxburgh, the national team's manager, was reluctant to disrupt the squad's preparations, but McNeill was not to be denied. 'Andy, if you don't let me talk to him, I'll make sure he can't play for you or anybody. If he wants to fuck me about, I'll fuck him about.' Once Roxburgh relented, McNeill stormed into the player's room and angrily accused Johnston of betraying him and the club. 'You mess me about and I'll fight you all the way,' McNeill said. 'I'll make sure you never fucking play again.'

The Celtic manager was so furious that he urged the board of directors to pay the rest of the transfer fee owed to Nantes, so that they would then own his registration and could force him out of the game. By now, Johnston was negotiating with Rangers, and although Souness claims no contact was made until after the Celtic deal fell through, both Butcher and Ally McCoist, Johnston's international room-mate, heard hints from the striker that he was considering a move to Ibrox – Johnston used to playfully say to McCoist that, 'Graeme Souness has some house, hasn't he? It's brilliant inside.' Money was a motivation, since Rangers were financially stronger than their Old Firm rivals, having redeveloped their stadium some years before clubs had been compelled by the Taylor Report that followed the Hillsborough disaster to spend the resources to make them all-seater; but so, too, was Johnston's chutzpah. Despite growing up a Celtic fan, and having understood his role as an idol for the Celtic support but also as a hate figure for Rangers fans – he crossed himself after being sent-off in an Old Firm game – the opportunity to be so brazen and heedless stirred him.

Souness is a charismatic figure, conceited but so self-assured that he appealed to Johnston's unabashed nature. Yet there was still an element of doubt in the striker's mind, a nagging uncertainty that prompted him to flee back to France and refuse to answer his phone for several days. It was not so much that he needed to be persuaded by Souness to make the move, but more that he had to take the time to come to terms with the enormity of what it would mean to turn his back on his former club and then sign for their oldest, fiercest rivals. If there was ever a moment when the deal – which would represent one of the great and brazen acts of oneupmanship in the history of the Old Firm – might flounder, this was it. Sensing that a final push was required, Souness flew to Paris, met Johnston at a pavement cafe near Orly airport, and the deal was signed. The Rangers manager kept the pen that they used, knowing the historical significance of the contract, but also that this was the gravest blow he could strike. Souness swept aside years of tradition at Ibrox (something that reflected old mindsets from other industries, when Catholics were told not to apply for jobs), while at the same time wounding Celtic, who lost out on a striker who was at the peak of his game, and who was revered by the fans. It was a transfer that epitomised the way that Rangers were moving purposefully and ambitiously into football's commercial age while their rivals dithered.

'Hurting Celtic was not the drive behind the deal. But yes, I knew it would be a consequence of the transfer,' Souness later reflected. 'I felt the manner of the move would damage them for a number of years. What was the chairman's reaction when I told him I wanted to sign Maurice? Disbelief. But within a minute we were all convinced that it was the right thing to do. It was done for all the right footballing reasons. That was all I was interested in. I was a lot younger at the time of the deal. None of the other stuff really bothered me. To be honest, a lot of that stuff was kept away from me. I only found out later all the different things that had happened. But at the time, I can honestly say I wasn't worried. I knew his quality and I knew he'd scored goals in different places throughout his career. The age was right and the money was right. The only problem for some people was his religion. You have to remember we weren't just signing a Roman Catholic – we were signing a Roman Catholic who had played for Celtic and who had posed with a Celtic strip on just a few weeks earlier. Mo had the full set of reasons not to make the move. That's why he deserves so much credit for going through with it. I can't say enough about Maurice in that respect. He had an attitude towards it that said, "Don't worry about it because I ain't worried about it and I'll make it happen." To be fair to him, he did make it happen and that spirit of his shone through. There was no fear with Maurice and that showed in his play too.'

Only a handful of people knew about the unfolding transfer, but it was also to change the dynamics of tabloid journalism in the country. The Scottish edition of the *Sun* was a small, dogged operation taking on the established might of the *Daily Record* when Jack Irvine, the editor, won a holiday to Majorca in a Press Fund lunch raffle. While away, he spent several evenings out with Souness, who alternated between asking Irvine's opinion about breaking Rangers' signing policy and being distracted by telephone calls. Irvine returned home on Saturday, 8 July believing something was stirring, then the following morning a sixteen-year-old boy on work experience asked to see him. He had been at his girlfriend's house when he saw a fax in her father's study with Johnston's name on it. The man did insurance for Rangers, and Irvine suddenly realised the story that had come his way. It was two o'clock in the afternoon, and he immediately phoned Souness, whose plane had just landed at Edinburgh airport.

'Those drunken dinners when you were asking me about signing a Catholic,' Irvine said. 'It's Mo Johnston, isn't it?'

'I'll phone you back,' Souness said, then hung up. An hour later, Irvine's phone rang. 'It's Graeme,' said the voice on the other end. 'Print it.'

The *Sun* ran with the news on its front page the following day, but there was still a sense of disbelief, of denial even, that such a transfer could take place, and other newspapers did not lift it and run it as their own story. This was something more than Rangers signing a high-profile Catholic footballer; it was the Ibrox club seeking out the player who had become not only synonymous with Celtic's ambition and sense of identity, but also the hate figure of the Rangers support, somebody who had scored goals in a successful Parkhead side, and become a talisman for the Celtic fans.

Even when Rangers called a press conference at Ibrox, journalists were expecting John Sheridan, the Republic of Ireland midfielder, to be revealed as the club's latest signing. Hours before, Johnston and McMurdo were hiding behind a cubicle door in the directors' toilet at Ibrox Stadium. Johnston had been shaving and smartening up his appearance when he and his agent were forced to suddenly hide from Doddie Soutar, the Rangers kitman, and a friend who came in to use the facilities. So they cowered behind a toilet door, panicking and trying to stifle their nervous laughter. 'They're getting things ready as if there is a signing. Who is it?' asked Soutar's friend. 'I don't care who it is, as long as it's not that Celtic bastard Johnston,' Soutar replied.

Johnston had doubted himself during the negotiations, but it was his fearless, almost insolent nature that pushed the deal through, and that saw him walk into the Blue Room at Ibrox later that day wearing a sheepish grin, while Souness looked on with stony defiance. 'First and foremost it was a football decision,' said David Murray, the chairman. 'We signed the player because he was the best Scottish player around and that is what mattered. Of course, it removed a cloud that hung above Rangers.' It was never revealed at the time, but Johnston made sure that there was a clause in his contract allowing him to walk away at any moment, but once the deal was signed, and the fierce response instigated, he was in his element: cocky and defiant.

Johnston later claimed that he could have accepted an approach from Montpellier – who signed Eric Cantona instead, after Johnston turned them down – and received more money than Rangers were paying him, and he also disputed that he had signed a contract with Celtic (although in effect it was a pre-contract agreement and Fifa eventually fined him £3,000 for reneging). McMurdo, too, says that the Celtic deal was not valid since it was his view that Nantes did not own Johnston's contract, but instead his registration was owned by a third-party company which he represented. McMurdo was banned from Celtic Park at the time, and so also claims that when Johnston told him he was travelling to Scotland to talk to McNeil, McMurdo made him take a letter stating that the striker could not sign any contract. More than twenty years later, the complexities of the deal remain vague, but the feelings have barely subsided – McNeil has spoken little more than a few words to Johnston in the intervening years, and is still irked by the Celtic board's refusal to pay the rest of the fee and allow them to ostracise the player for what he saw as a betrayal of his club.

Glasgow reacted to the transfer with a typical show of aggressive posturing and dark humour. Rangers fans gathered outside Ibrox to protest, and some even burned their scarves and season tickets for the watching press photographers, while one fan staged a sit-in at the turnstiles. A hearse stopped outside and a wreath was laid mourning '116 Years of Tradition', while a handful of Union flags were raised bearing a 'No Mo Here' message, but there was not the outcry that was anticipated. For Celtic supporters, the transfer hurt like an act of treachery. They loathed Johnston, and for much of his time at Rangers he was accompanied by six bodyguards working a rota system – including one, Big George, who followed him almost everywhere – while the club even hired a bomb disposal squad to protect the players' cars during a house party that they attended. At one stage after the transfer, there were even reports of Johnston's father having been attacked. McMurdo was assigned a bodyguard for six months after the transfer, and being a Rangers fan himself, he later earned the mocking nickname, Agent Orange. Among Celtic supporters, Johnston became known as Judas, with his portrait in Baird's Bar – a renowned Celtic pub – having a blue nose painted on it. A Celtic supporters' group based in Motherwell also wrote to the club asking for permission to change their name to the We Hate Maurice Johnston Celtic Supporters' Club. The feeling among them was of being distraught, but also anger and fear, the sense that a great shift of power had occurred, leaving their side behind. Rangers were able to outspend them and be more boldly ambitious, and the moral authority that Celtic had claimed for so long – signing players of any faith and considering their club's background as one of persecution compared to the prejudice of the Protestant community that Rangers represented – was also slipping.

But there was an air of farce to much of the reaction once the initial indignation – on both sides – had diminished. Andy Cameron, the comedian and Rangers fan, was presenting a cheque at a Glasgow school when the story broke, and the janitor said to him: 'I dunno where he's going to live . . . he'll need to get a hold of that Salman Rushdie's hoose.' A Celtic fan, Nan O'Malley, also received death threats addressed to her dog, which was called Mo. A quip that quickly did the rounds of the city's drinking establishments and workplaces was: 'Forgive me father, for I have signed', which captured the religious element of the transfer, but also satirised it.

To find respite from the torrent of attention, Johnston lived in a house in Edinburgh owned by Souness, but threats, intimidation, and broken windows at other properties he owned or that his parents lived in, were commonplace. He also had to integrate with the Rangers squad, many of whom had grown up with the club's traditions, or embraced them on arrival at Ibrox – it was Souness and Terry Butcher who hung portraits of the Queen in the home dressing room.

After signing, Johnston flew to Italy where the squad were doing their pre-season training at the Tuscan resort of Il Ciocco, arriving at the complex by helicopter. It was lunchtime, and the Rangers players were sitting, as usual, at a long dining table. A smaller one was set-up in the corner, for one person, with only bread and water on it. Johnston was told to sit on his own, like a pariah, and only realised it was a joke when all the players started laughing. Butcher also recollects Jimmy Bell, the club's kitman, refusing to wash Johnston's training gear, but the general response was one of acceptance, or even admiration for his courage. 'I don't think anybody else could have done it. It was very brave,' said Richard Gough, the Rangers defender. 'Mo was a good lad so there was never bitterness among the players.' As he did on international duty, Johnston roomed with McCoist, and one afternoon after a training session, they went for a sleep. With the wooden shutters drawn, the room was pitch black, and Johnston was still on edge from the threats that had been made in the hours following his transfer, with McCoist having joked that if an attacker broke in then he was worried he would be mistaken for Johnston. When McCoist woke suddenly from his sleep, he saw a shadow move across the doorway, and he started to scream in terror. Then another voice began to holler, and when the light was eventually switched on, Johnston was curled up in the corner of the room with his hands over his head. He had been making his way to the toilet when he heard McCoist shouting, and had panicked that somebody had broken in. The players wound Johnston up about his Celtic background and the furore his signing caused back in Scotland, but there was also an acknowledgment that the club had bought a talented and accomplished striker, who would also be the centre of attention, taking the pressure off the rest of the squad.

Souness was certain that signing Johnston was right for the team, and necessary for the club. But it turned out that the vast majority of the Rangers support could accept the deal for what it was: progress, a smart football move and an act of wilful superiority over Celtic. Of the Rangers fans who returned their season tickets on hearing of the transfer, many later ruefully asked for them back, or claimed that they had lost them. A hard core of fans would never accept Johnston – for being a Catholic but also for being a former Celtic player who had inflicted pain on them; and a story is often told about a supporters' club that years later worked out results and league tables for Rangers that disregarded all of Johnston's goals. The striker himself later admitted that he was always aware of a small background noise of resentment that he would never overcome. But once the season started, and he began to play with an immediate sense of assurance and determination, the majority of the Rangers fans were won over.

His first Old Firm game was at Celtic Park, a 0–0 draw in which Johnston was the focus of derision and wrath, a hatefulness that he toiled against. His second was at Ibrox, on 4 November 1989, and he scored a late winning goal with a true strike of the ball. He had only registered his first goal for the club in the previous game, but suddenly Johnston's potential as a significant player, and a source of aggravation for Celtic, became clear to the Rangers support; they celebrated him, and while it could never be an unreserved acclaim for some, the ovations for Johnston became a riposte to justified criticism of the club's Protestant-only signing tradition. 'The fans had been thinking, "Does this guy ever want to score?" But I knew my time would come, and when it did, I seized the moment,' Johnston said. 'Afterwards, I walked into the dressing room, and there was a different respect. When I came out, I walked past the marble staircase, out through the front door, and everything had just lifted. All the shit was finished. I could have told the security guards to scram there and then. After three or four months it was no problem. I was scoring goals and enjoying my football. The odd problem cropped up. Stones would be thrown at my parents' house and I'd get things chucked at my car. My own stupidity didn't help things. I'd answer back if someone shouted at me in the street when I should have kept my mouth shut. I'm proud of what I achieved by signing for Rangers. I opened the door for Catholic footballers to sign and take satisfaction from that. I made it easier for players to go there. Things moved on.'

Johnston was a success at Rangers, scoring forty-six goals in a hundred games, twice winning the league and earning several individual player of the year awards from supporters' groups. One was from the Moodiesburn Loyal, whose president was Doddie Soutar, the Rangers kitman Johnston and McMurdo had hidden from in the Ibrox toilet. And it was Soutar who introduced the player at the awards night, then presented him with his trophy.

But the controversy has never lost its edge. Some Celtic supporters still refuse to speak his name, while others stalk him on the internet, using messageboards to threaten and abuse him. When a charity match between former Rangers and Celtic players was due to be held some years ago, and Johnston proposed playing one half for each side, he was forced to pull out because Celtic supporters were threatening to boycott the game. Yet Johnston has twin sons, T.J. and Tyler, one of whom supports Rangers and the other Celtic. Johnston's own father was a Rangers supporter, and it was his Catholic mother who encouraged his boyhood love of Celtic. He has now found peace and a certain perspective from living in America then Canada, having ended his playing career in Major League Soccer and moved into coaching, but Johnston declines most requests to talk about his Old Firm careers, preferring instead to let the story provide its own meaning.

Rangers now regularly sign Catholic players without the issue being raised, with some like Jorg Albertz, Lorenzo Amoruso, Rino Gattuso and Shota Arveladze becoming cult heroes (and all of whom developed their own sentimental attachment to the club

and the fans, despite the obvious anti-Catholic rhetoric of some
of the terrace songs). Paul Le Guen, a French Catholic, also
managed the club, although his reign is not fondly remembered
since results were poor and he struggled to understand the
mentality of the Scottish players. Celtic never refused to sign a
player because of his religion, having always taken great pride in
their all-inclusive policy (a reaction, no doubt, to the feeling of
persecution felt by Catholics in Scotland when the club was
formed). Jock Stein, the legendary Celtic manager, would often
target Protestant signings first, particularly among young players,
because he always knew that Rangers would not be interested in
any Catholics. Stein himself was a Protestant who was raised as a
Rangers fan, but who railed against any notion of bigotry, while
many of the club's most revered players, such as Kenny Dalglish
and Danny McGrain, also grew up as Protestant Rangers fans.

Yet neither group of supporters can claim to be unblemished.
Mark Walters, the black English winger, was pelted by bananas
thrown from the Celtic Park terraces when he made his Old Firm
debut there for Rangers. John Spencer, a Catholic who signed for
Rangers as a schoolboy, also tells of being abused at school and
challenged to fights by fellow pupils. A friend even threatened him
while the pair were watching an Old Firm game together and
Spencer celebrated Rangers scoring. For players coming into the
Old Firm rivalry from outside Scotland, it can often be an unset-
tling experience.

'I remember in my first few weeks there were all kinds of rumours
going round and I'd be asked by Rangers fans which school I had
been to and what my parents' names were,' said Terry Butcher. 'I
didn't say. I simply told them I was an English footballer. It eventually came out [that] I was Church of England. I recall one incident
at Ipswich before a reserve game when I crossed myself, something
I'd seen Alan Brazil do. Big Allan Hunter [a Northern Ireland

international] was sitting in the stand and after the game he grabbed me and asked me if I was a Catholic. I told him I wasn't. I was an English Protestant. Why, then, he asked, did I cross myself? I told him it was for luck but he told me to remember I was a Protestant and warned me never to do it again – if I did, he would really sort me out.

'I quickly forgot about it, but my arrival in Scotland soon reminded me – and then some. This thing went far beyond religion. It is more than a passion, it is a way of life, and there is nothing like it down south. It can be very intoxicating as well as weird, spooky, strange and scary. Initially, it was just a case of getting used to it. Rangers and Celtic have hundreds of supporters' clubs all over Glasgow, Scotland and the world, and they all have award ceremonies for their own player of the year. They were such warm, generous people, but you couldn't just go for an hour. There were flute bands too and they would have you up on the stage singing the usual party songs, which I learned quickly. The first Rangers supporters' club I went to was in Larkhall and I was asked to sing a Rangers song. I tried to explain that, as I had only arrived, I hadn't had time to learn any. There was one thing I knew about Glasgow Rangers. Allan Hunter had taught me the phrase "No surrender" and, with those two words, I brought the house down. Old Firm games do something to you – they turn you into a different person. At times I became someone I didn't like. I'm normally a placid bloke, but my senses totally left me. Yet until you have played in an Old Firm game, you can have no idea the effect they have on you. Potentially, they are the best in the world. But they can also be the worst. And definitely the most volatile. They are extremely frightening because you carry the responsibilities of your set of fans. And these fans often expect far too much. At times there is no way you can live up to those expectations – and you react in a way that is totally out of character.'

The ball's there, it's mine, fuck. I caught him there, that was a bad one. Fuck it, he needs to know I'm not messing around. 'I was going for the ball ref, the ball. No, my studs weren't up, it's just the way I stretched for the ball. And it's my first foul, the first one of the game. You can't book me for that.' I got away with that one, the gaffer would've been fucking raging if I was sent off. Still, those fucking fans shouting and bawling, I'll show them if I get a chance. I'd love to score in this game, then I'd give it right fucking back to them. Right in their faces. Yeh, that would be something. Imagine their faces. And imagine our boys, they'd be going mental. I'd be the man then, no shitty comments from anybody after that. I'd be untouchable, they'd love me then, all of them.

Got to stay on the park, though. No more daft challenges. That fucker really does my head in, though, arrogant bastard. Thinks he's right better than me. Him and their fans. If he starts any shit, I'll be right in his face. No backing down, not today. We really need to start playing some football here, or this game's going nowhere. How long to go? This result's all right, but a win would be special, they'd really be fucked then. And we'd be the ones. No doubt about it. The fucking ones.

In his innocence and eagerness to fit in, Terry Butcher was not alone among the players who moved to Rangers in the decade after Graeme Souness changed the scale of Rangers' ambition. In July 1995, Paul Gascoigne moved to Ibrox from Lazio in a £4.3m transfer that was sealed after Walter Smith, the Rangers manager, bumped into Gascoigne on the beach during a holiday. The midfielder was, by then, still considered to be within touching distance of the best of his talent, the kind of chutzpah he showed during the 1990 World Cup, when he was one of England's best players on their journey to the semi-final. It was the tears that Gascoigne could not contain during that game against West Germany, when he received a booking that ruled him out of the final, that both endeared him to the English nation but also enhanced the character that he had become: Gazza, the clowning figure whose emotions were uninhibited but who was also capable of moments of brilliance on the football field. He had failed to settle in Rome, while his career had been dogged by a cruciate ligament injury suffered during the 1991 FA Cup final against Nottingham Forest (and one that was self-inflicted, after Gascoigne launched a reckless challenge on Gary Charles). But Gascoigne was still one of British football's most high-profile and, on occasion, talented footballers, and his arrival represented a coup for Smith. After signing his contract, Gascoigne stepped outside the main doors at Ibrox to be greeted by a throng of supporters. The midfielder was sporting a cropped, peroxide blond haircut that immediately became popular with Rangers fans throughout the city, but he brought with his undoubted talent that sense of being a manic, sometimes impulsive character.

Even Ian Ferguson could not foresee the furore that Gascoigne would provoke. A Glaswegian who grew up supporting the club – and who reflected more than most players the sense of hostility within the Old Firm divide – Ferguson suggested to his new English teammate that he should mimic playing a flute on the Ibrox pitch. The pair were talking in the dressing room before Gascoigne's first game for the club in 1995, against Steaua Bucharest in a pre-season tournament. 'You should run in front of the fans and kid on you are playing the flute,' Ferguson told him. 'They will take it as a bit of a laugh and they will really appreciate it.' Gascoigne was already called Ticker by the other players, a nickname based on the phrase: tick-tock, tick-tock, tick-tock . . . boom, and his tendency to be involved in dramas that suddenly blow up around him. In the forty-fifth minute of the game, Gascoigne scored with a simple tap-in, and then turned to the Rangers fans and pretended to play the flute, which represents the marchers who take part in Orange Walks in the west of Scotland and Northern Ireland. 'He wis playin' in an Orange Walk band,' said Mick Martin, a Rangers fan, after the game. 'Brilliant. That's what we're aw aboot.' Yet as much as the Ibrox supporters revelled in Gascoigne's display, and the club sought to emphasise to him how serious his misdemeanour was by fining him two weeks' wages, it took outside intervention to reveal the extent of the divide in the city he had moved to. A week after the incident, Gascoigne was sitting in a traffic jam when a car pulled up alongside him. The driver motioned to the player to lower his window, then told him: 'I wouldn't do that again, mate.'

'Why not?' Gascoigne replied.

'Because I'll slit your throat next time.'

As Gascoigne laughed nervously, the man slowly ran his finger along his throat, before driving off. 'Looking back it was utter madness on my behalf,' said Ferguson. 'I could have ended up getting him killed – it was that bad. He was raging and rightly so.'

Gascoigne came to realise the significance of symbolism and the religious nature of the Old Firm rivalry, but he could not restrain his own impulsive behaviour. His first season was a success, and on the field he generally tended to excel, but life was always troubled for a man who suffered from depression, anxiety, obsessive-compulsive disorder and an inability to relax or fill time on his own. He was never truly at ease with himself, and the tensions of Glasgow only exacerbated this restlessness. On 2 January 1998, while warming up behind the goal as a substitute at Celtic Park, Gascoigne was verbally abused by the home fans, and eventually responded. He turned to them and pretended again to play the flute, with the gesture seen by many people in the stadium as well as being captured on the live television coverage. The reaction was furious, and this time the Englishman could not claim ignorance to the meaning of his gesture. Although he later apologised, a television viewer complained to Strathclyde Police, who launched an investigation, as did the Scottish Football Association, with Rangers again fining the player and then donating the money to charity.

This time, the aftermath saw Gascoigne receive 126 threats, including a handwritten letter from Ireland, in Gaelic, warning him to 'watch his back' and detailing much of his daily routine. The player was terrified, as the author of the letter claimed to be writing on behalf of the IRA. Gascoigne immediately took the letter to Govan police station, who traced it to a man in Dublin, but they were unable to prosecute him unless he set foot in the UK. Instead, they showed Gascoigne how to open his mail safely and to check under his car for bombs. Although Gascoigne's friend, the DJ and television presenter Chris Evans tried to make light of the situation by sending the footballer a T-shirt with a target on the front, for six months Gascoigne fretted about his safety, moving out of the lodge in Loch Lomond that he had made his home and turning increasingly to drink to escape the sense of his life unravelling. He sent his two cars – a Range Rover and a convertible Mercedes-Benz – to England, and rented four different chalets, at a cost of £15,000 a month each, so that he could randomly vary where he slept. His lifelong friend, Jimmy 'Five Bellies' Gardner, continued to act as his driver, but they used hire cars and changed them on a regular basis.

Then the police came to visit, to tell him that the man in Dublin had phoned them to say that the threat was rescinded. But by then Gascoigne was more and more lost to the alcohol and erratic behaviour that was to lead to his departure from his Ibrox in 1998. He was a fragile character, capable of genius on the football field, but self-destructive and often hapless off it. Gascoigne was needy and often infantile in his behaviour, qualities that made him vulnerable in a city like Glasgow, where weakness tends to be met with disdain. The player lacked self-awareness, and while playing for Middlesbrough in a testimonial match for Alan McLaren, the Rangers defender, in 1999, Gascoigne repeated the flute gesture again. The Englishman was guilty of immaturity, certainly, and struggled with a reckless, self-destructive streak, although much of this behaviour was later explained by the revelation in his autobiography of the traumas of his childhood and the troubled mental state they resulted in. At first, he did not fully understand the nature of the Old Firm divide, seeing it only as a football rivalry rather than something that reflects but also influences tensions in society. Any footballer or manager with a streak of arrogance can set out to irritate opposition fans – while manager of Galatasaray, Graeme Souness placed a large club flag in the centre of their city rival's Fenerbahce's pitch after winning the Turkish cup final, which almost caused a riot – but in Glasgow such gestures would carry a greater impact.

Artur Boruc joined Celtic in 2005 from the Polish side Legia Warsaw as a goalkeeper with international experience and a reputation for occasional lapses in behaviour. In August 2006, he crossed himself in front of Rangers fans at Ibrox during an Old Firm game, then laughed at them and motioned with both hands for them to 'come ahead'. Police officers later claimed that it took ten minutes to calm down the situation in the stands. Like many footballers, Boruc crosses himself as a matter of habit or faith as he runs onto the field at the beginning of the first and second-halves of games, but the direct goading of the Rangers fans that accompanied the gesture was deliberate, and it exposed the angst that gathers around so much of Scotland's attitude towards the religious rivalry of the Old Firm. Following complaints from Rangers supporters, Strathclyde Police submitted a report of the incident to the Procurator Fiscal, and six months later Boruc was cautioned for breach of the peace, with the formal warning coming for behaviour that 'provoked alarm and crowd trouble'.

The Catholic Church reacted with indignation, describing the caution as an 'alarming development, especially since the sign of the cross is globally accepted as a gesture of religious reverence. It is extremely regrettable that Scotland seems to have made itself one of the few countries in the world where this simply religious gesture is considered an offence'. Alex Salmond, then the leader of the Scottish National Party in opposition at the Scottish Parliament, demanded an explanation from the Fiscal, who later clarified the caution by saying it was 'based on an assessment of behaviour, not one single act, which appeared to be directed towards the crowd, which was being incited by that behaviour'. So Boruc placed himself in the midst of the enduring tension of the Old Firm's rivalry, its religious language and expression, and Scottish society's uneasiness at dealing with the complexities of this relationship between the clubs. Waving Union Jack or Irish tricolour flags at Old Firm games cannot be considered inflammatory, and many players have blessed themselves without being cautioned or causing trouble, including Rangers players, yet Boruc then proceeded to compound his gesture by stirring the Rangers fans with his invitation for them to attack him. Although his agent claimed it was merely an act of Boruc's faith, what he did after blessing himself was seen as incitement. Yet any nuance was lost as the Church, politicians, the criminal authorities and football agonised over the events, and asserted a point of view shaped by their own agenda.

He became known among the Celtic fans as the Holy Goalie, yet Boruc, like Gascoigne, could not contain the antagonistic part of his nature, or at least not fail to respond to his hounding by Rangers supporters, who routinely booed him. In an Old Firm game at Celtic Park in April 2008, which the home side won 3–2, Boruc removed his goalkeeper's jersey after the final whistle to reveal a T-shirt that bore a picture of the late Pope John Paul II and the words, 'God Bless the Pope', which prompted the Democratic Unionist MP for East Londonderry, Gregory Campbell, to propose a parliamentary motion that expressed support for the work carried out to combat sectarianism by Rangers and Celtic but that deeply regretted the actions of the Celtic goalkeeper Artur Boruc.

That's it, all over. Thank God. A draw, could be better, but at least we didn't lose the game. That would have been disastrous. I'm fucked, my legs are empty, there's nothing left. I wish I'd taken that chance, but it's gone now. 'Well played. Well played. You too, mate. Aye, well played.' Survived it. A couple of shaky moments, but I did okay. I can't be hung out for anything by those fucking journalists. What do they know? The gaffer should be all right, too, I did everything he asked. Kept the head, too.

Got to go over to the fans, show some appreciation. Look at them all, still here, still singing. It's crazy. Some'll be out tonight. I wonder if I should go out for a drink? I should be all right, no hassle, surely. Could be a good night, plenty of folk wanting to hang out. But then maybe it's safer just to stay at home, sit it out just for tonight. There are some crazy bastards out there. I mean, look at them. I need to get inside, up the tunnel, into the dressing room. No bother, no hassles, just back inside. Away from it, the noise. Away from it.

Other Old Firm players have been more curious about the historic divide between Celtic and Rangers. The Norwegian striker, Harald Brattbakk, attempted to come to terms with the religious nature of a football rivalry he found more intense than anything he had experienced. After signing for Celtic in 1997, he read about the background of the relationship between the two clubs. 'It was amazing. I don't think I realised how important the game is, how big it is,' he said. 'I could sense the feeling in the dressing room, I could sense the supporters and everything around the game before it. It was huge. I had a good experience playing in big games for Rosenborg, but the Old Firm is like nothing else. I've told people who go to see *El Clásico* in Spain, or the Manchester derby, that if they want to see a real derby, they should go to Glasgow. I played against a lot of big clubs in Europe, but the Old Firm is beyond everything. I had to find out what it was. I didn't know that the emotions could be so strong and that religion was such a big part of the game. In terms of getting a good Old Firm game, it's positive, but I remember a kid being killed on his way home from Ibrox. He was just going through the wrong neighbourhood on his way home, wearing a Celtic strip, and he was killed. That's not acceptable. I'm a Christian myself, but I don't treat Muslims, Catholics or whatever any differently, I let people have their beliefs, and it's sometimes too bad when it becomes a part of sport.'

While playing for Celtic in 1998, the Danish defender Marc Rieper travelled to Buncrana, a small town in Donegal, to help to carry the coffin of Oran Doherty. The eight-year-old boy was one of the twenty-eight victims of the Omagh Bomb, and he was an avid Celtic supporter, even being buried in the team's strip. 'That was the saddest day of my life,' Rieper said soon after returning to Glasgow. 'I was asked by the family to attend Oran's funeral, and my immediate response was yes. There were 10,000 people there, including all the politicians. All for a wee boy who was buried in his Celtic strip. A Celtic flag was on his coffin. That was how much the club meant to the wee boy. Some things go beyond football. Certainly, that day put life into perspective. It was so sad. I spoke to the family afterwards, and they said they were very grateful. I suppose, if I could help them in any small way, then it was right I was there.

'I played in London derbies with West Ham, and you cannot compare them. The Old Firm is different to any other game in the world. People will say the Milan derby is better, but there is more to Glasgow's one than football. That is something we have to live with. It doesn't make it right, but it won't change, no matter who is on the pitch. The supporters look at it differently. For them, it is the biggest thing in football, and it is a fantastic occasion, but we need to put it into perspective and not make it more than it really is.'

Foreign players can sometimes struggle to accept the sheer scale of the Old Firm rivalry, what it means and what it expects of them. When Rangers lost 5–1 to Celtic in November 1998, Ian Ferguson, who grew up near Celtic Park in an area famous for its staunch support of the Ibrox side, embarked on a furious rant in the dressing room afterwards. He felt that the foreign players signed the previous summer by Dick Advocaat, the Dutch manager, in his first season in charge did not understand what the game represented, and his rebukes were fearsome. The foreign players all came from clubs that could accept losing a match, because the points could always be regained in the next game. But in Scotland, for the Old Firm, the culture is of winning, and especially of being dominant over your city rivals. The following day at training, the Dutch international full-back Arthur Numan, an experienced and senior member of the squad but also one of the newcomers after joining from PSV Eindhoven, said privately to Ferguson that he felt the midfielder had been harsh. Ferguson's response was another tirade about the importance of the game, which Numan eventually came to understand.

'Although I am a Catholic I never had any problems with them being the Protestant club,' said Jorg Albertz, the German midfielder who became a great hero of the Rangers fans for his commitment and goals against Celtic. 'Among the foreign players it is first of all the performance which counts. As I played really well right from the start, I was accepted by the fans. This relationship turned into something like love – I have never had a better relation with the fans than I had with the Rangers loyals. It doesn't get better than that.'

Even the final whistle does not bring respite from the strains of the Old Firm rivalry, with players wary of socialising after a defeat, or being careful which restaurant or nightclub they visit after a victory. Glasgow can be a sullen, edgy place after a Rangers v. Celtic game, with all of the violence that once agitated the terraces now displaced to pubs, streets and homes across the city and beyond. The players experience the same extreme emotions, of triumph in victory and despair in defeat, but they also become targets for supporters. The losers do not like to see opposition players out celebrating, nor their own players, who they feel should be too wracked by sorrow to leave the house. Billy McNeill and Tommy Burns used to advise Celtic players to avoid Glasgow in the aftermath of Old Firm games, since there was too much danger of encountering situations that were outwith the players' control. Yet Andy Walker, the Celtic striker, did not follow McNeill's advice, and after a 1–0 win at Celtic Park in his Old Firm debut in August 1987, he joined his friends on a trip to a Glasgow nightclub. As he ordered a round at the bar, Walker included a lager tops for himself. 'Is that for you,' the barman asked.

'Yeah, that's mine,' said Walker, as he opened his wallet to pay.

The barman then spat in his pint before charging for the drinks. Walker immediately left the club and went straight into a taxi home. He was to encounter other incidents during his Celtic career, including being out for a drink when a man came up to him to say, 'You're in the wrang pub,' before dropping a full pint glass on the floor at his feet, and the night he was out with Derek Whyte, a Celtic teammate, when a man in a smart suit walked up to Whyte and, unprovoked, punched him in the face, before stamping on him then walking away.

The game is capable of creating heroes and villains in the simple narrative of sporting achievement, but what distinguishes the Old Firm rivalry is Glasgow's mixture of religious intolerance, football obsessiveness, and aggressive, macho behaviour. There is also no place to hide, even for those players innocent of the mistakes of Gascoigne, the controversies of Boruc, or the sheer, headstrong shamelessness of Johnston. It is, in many ways, a game that is indifferent to the players who are taking part, because it is the rivalry that matters, even beyond the sporting consequence of the outcome. If one side has already won the league and there is an Old Firm match, it remans frenzied and full-blooded, even though the points at stake are meaningless. At times, it is a spectacle, something more than a football match, and closer instead to a way of life.

CHAPTER 2

THE REFEREE INTERVENES

Watches, both of them, working. Cards, red and yellow, back pocket, top pocket. Notebook, pencil, coin. Whistle. Check my watch, 12.30 p.m. Eleven players on both sides. Assistants in place. Where's the signal from the television official? Okay. Okay. Here we go.

Every challenge is a confrontation. Four fouls in three minutes: Rangers No. 27, Kyle Lafferty, on Celtic No. 2, Andreas Hinkel, twenty-three seconds played; Celtic No. 46, Aiden McGeady, on Rangers No. 21, Kirk Broadfoot – those two will be on the edge all day, I need to keep on top of that. Rangers No. 9, Kris Boyd, on Celtic No. 5, Gary Caldwell – I'll need to watch that pair, too; Celtic No. 9, Georgios Samaras, on Rangers No. 16, Steven Whittaker. This is relentless. That's a Samaras handball. And a foul by Rangers No. 27, Kyle Lafferty. Where's the captains, David Weir and Gary Caldwell? They need to calm this down; it's so frantic. 'No handball, that wasn't deliberate. Yell in my face like that again, Barry, and you'll be in the book.' What's that booing? It's the Celtic fans. What now? Novo. What happened to him, why's he on the ground? I never saw that. 'Nacho, what's wrong? What's the injury? Do you need treatment? Physio, come on.' Right, what's going on behind me? The noise, it's so loud. Only eight minutes gone. Both watches still working. Cards, notebook, pencil, whistle. What next? 'Okay, make the change.' Rangers No. 10 off, and No. 2 on: Maurice Edu. This noise.

Here we go again. What now? Lafferty. That's handball. He's too wound up. 'Give the ball back, Kyle, and calm down. I'm watching you. Behave.' It's all Celtic here, Rangers are under pressure, they'll react. Trip. Foul, Rangers No. 27, Kyle Lafferty, on Celtic No. 11, Danny Fox. Lafferty again. 'Last warning, Kyle, you'll be in the book next time, I'm warning you. I won't take it.' Rangers No. 6, Lee McCulloch, down, head knock. 'Stop. You okay, Lee? Take your time.' Another foul, Rangers No. 2, Maurice Edu, on Celtic No. 9, Georgios Samaras; free kick to Celtic. 'Wait until I blow the whistle. Wait.' Who's that jostling in the penalty area? Watch them. 'Take the kick.' Watch them. No. Foul. Foul. Celtic. That was a foul. Celtic No. 10. Fortune. I saw him barge the goalkeeper. 'No. No goal. It was a foul. Arm, he hit the goalkeeper's arm. Walk. Walk away. Walk. Free kick. No goal.'

That's the one. That's the decision. I'll be hung out for that one, whatever the final score. Dammit. I'm sure he knocked the goalkeeper's arm out of the way. I'll know at half time, somebody will text me. What if I made a mistake? What if that was a goal? I don't want to know then. No, I'm sure of it, certain. I know what I saw. I did see it, didn't I? He hit the goalkeeper's arm, and knocked it out of the way. Didn't he? Oh Christ, I hope I was right.

The referee knows six days before that he will take charge of the Old Firm game, when the Scottish Football Association announces the match officials for the following weekend. It is the game that every referee wants to be awarded, its high profile and volatile nature distinguishing it, so that it is a sign of status; only the best individuals can be granted the responsibility, and there is competition among the referees for who is appointed, who takes charge of more of them, and who is granted the responsibility for the major ones, the cup finals and the critical league fixtures.

The build-up begins almost two weeks before, with the game written about in the newspapers every day and talked about on the radio stations every evening. Steve Conroy is the referee for the Celtic v. Rangers game of 3 January 2010, the first time he has been allocated an Old Firm derby, and he is aware of all the coverage, because he has to be. Everything feeds into the game: its context – Rangers' lead in the league, Celtic's desperation not to lose, and Tony Mowbray, the Celtic manager, being under pressure, having been defeated in the first Old Firm game of the season at Ibrox – but also the comments of managers and players. A pointed or antagonistic remark during the days running up to the game can then be retaliated against once it kicks off. The referee has to be aware of everything, but particularly his role as the one restraint on the game, the figure who is expected to control it and manage it.

He needs to know the personalities of those involved: which players are likely to be aggressive and hostile; which players can be talked to reasonably; which ones you need to be stern with, or warn constantly about their behaviour; and who needs to be watched on the two benches. Where are all the potential flashpoints? The referee, wherever he is from, is aware of all the nuances around the derby match, the back-story of the current teams and individuals, who is feeling the tension more, which players thrive and which become more agitated, which ones play up to their own supporters, and are scorned by the other side. But the referee is known, too; his family, where he lives, where he went to school, what his religious background is. So he becomes pigeonholed in the minds of supporters, who see bias in every decision: he's one of them. Although in truth they never see the match official as one of their own.

As the game approaches, the referee becomes more aware of the way it seeps into his life. In the newspapers and on the airwaves, former referees talk about their experiences in Rangers v. Celtic games, the moments that spilled out of control and the disputes they generated, and speculate how he will handle his first Old Firm match. 'Steve looks comfortable in the fixtures that really matter,' wrote Kenny Clark, a former grade one referee, in his newspaper column. 'I can't give him a greater compliment. He's been involved in plenty of controversy in recent years. If you're going to referee the top games and make big decisions, then you will make headlines and you will be regarded as controversial. It's the nature of the beast. If you are not going to be big and brave, and be prepared to run the risk of unwanted headlines, you can't do the job.'

Days before the game Conroy, a 43-year-old doctor who lives in Lanarkshire, works in an addiction unit and has been on the SFA's senior referee list for ten years, meets Hugh Dallas, the SFA's head of refereeing, and his deputy John Fleming at Hampden for a coffee and some informal advice about how to handle the game, and what to expect. It is Dallas, who took charge of twenty Old Firm fixtures himself, who makes the decision about which referee is assigned to which game. 'Of course, I'll be nervous,' Conroy said after learning of his appointment. 'But I'm like that before every game. And, yes, I've been thinking a lot about it, again that's something I do before each match. I was quite old when I started compared to referees today, I was twenty-seven. It was a Sunday morning boys' match at Bishopbriggs and a wee guy on the touchline told me I was set for a slashing if his mates' team didn't win. I patted him on the head and got on with it. I was surprised and pleased to be picked for this [Old Firm] game. It's an honour and hopefully an inspiration to others who are too old to be on the Fifa list. I like to talk my way through games, and the man-management involved in my day job helps, but it's not just me as the ref that's involved in incidents – players must take responsibility. You just have to accept the presence [of television cameras] and get on with it. You make decisions honestly from your angle and you go with them.'

The casual guidance from superiors, or more experienced colleagues, has become something of a ritual, a way for referees to hand down their knowledge, to try to exert their own influence on the game, as though it might be controlled through collaboration, even if there is only one referee, two assistants and a fourth official, isolated, on the day itself. When Conroy met Dallas and Fleming in their modest but well-ordered office at Hampden, he learned of their experiences of the Old Firm game, how it can be stopped from rearing out of control, and how to handle the sheer frenzy of the occasion.

'Bed your way into the game,' Dallas says to him, still a stern figure, his narrow eyes carrying the flicker of a rebuke. 'But expect that crunching tackle early doors and deal with it with a disciplinary sanction. If there's not a lot of malice in it, and you can ride it by speaking to the player, then fine, but just give what you see. With 60,000 fans screaming at you, you've got to be strong enough to shut it out and address each decision as it comes along. Do plenty of talking to the captains, tell them beforehand that you'll be looking for their help during the game, so that they're level-headed. The laws of the game don't change because it's the Old Firm, you've just got to work harder. Be very strong and no matter how unbalanced you feel things are at the time – if the fouls are all going against one team – if you think you're doing the right thing then stick by it, don't try to balance it up. After the game, trust me, you'll be more mentally exhausted than you will be physically. I don't know who's going to win, I don't know who's going to score, but the one thing I do know is that you'll get the blame. When a team loses, they tend to attack the referee. You've got to be prepared for that.'

Dallas carries himself with the erect posture of a man used to asserting himself by his mere presence. His ruddy features are a little rounder than they were when he was at the height of his career, but he still carries an air of authority. Referees either shrink from the exposure that comes with their position, or embrace it, and Dallas has always been comfortable with the presence of the media in his life. For a time, he was one of the most recognisable officials in British football, and he is always quick to reach for an anecdote about his friendship with the world-renowned former referee Pierluigi Collina. Yet Dallas was also valued enough by Fifa to be named as fourth official at the 2002 World Cup final between Brazil and Germany. Wearing a suit and sitting in an office inside Hampden from where the refereeing department is run, the sense is still of a man used to being obeyed.

In his first Old Firm game, a 3–3 draw at Ibrox in November 1995, Dallas booked eight players, wrongly disallowed a goal for Rangers and at one stage was grappling with Andy Goram, the Rangers goalkeeper, in the six-yard box while holding back John Hughes, the giant Celtic defender. Kenny Clark, another leading referee during his career, once had the badge ripped off his black jersey while separating Rangers and Celtic players. The Old Firm game demands that referees are imposing not only in their judgement and authority but also physically, as if they almost single-handedly control the mood of the match and influence its every movement.

'Dick Advocaat [the former Rangers manager] was a great guy for coming out and saying, "We're really pleased with the refereeing appointment today, he is a top ref,"' says Dallas. 'That didn't wash with me, that was just to have a go at Celtic, who wouldn't be long in telling you that. So the first chance I got to go to the Rangers dugout during the game, I'd dress him down. I was asking him where he'd been on holiday or something, but as far as everybody was concerned, he was getting a dressing down. It's gamesmanship.'

In the build-up to the match, neighbours, workmates, acquaintances, even strangers in everyday encounters, all talk about the same, sole topic. 'How will the Old Firm game go?' 'You'll look after our team, won't you?' 'You keep a rein on them, you've got to watch out for that wee bugger.' There is no haven; even at home, where the door can be shut on the crowding attention, because the mind is still a collision of quandaries. What will happen in the match? How will I handle it? What if I lose control of it all? What then? What if there is a mass brawl, or a player loses control? What if I make a mistake, something that influences the outcome of the game, a penalty or a red card? What then? I'll be crucified, by everybody.

For two or three nights before an Old Firm match, Dallas often barely slept, and on the morning of the game he rose sharply at 6 a.m. He was always thinking about what could happen, the consequences of an error of judgement, of the inevitable pillorying of his reputation. The actions of the managers and the players exert a greater influence on the outcome, but the referee alone is the public scapegoat, for both teams, their managers, the media, and both sets of supporters. 'Your family is affected by it because you've got children who go to school [and are confronted by it],' Dallas says. 'That doesn't happen with any other game.'

After rising, Dallas would take a walk, often with his dog, Charlie, to try to clear his mind and compose himself, and think through the routine of the occasion, but also the scenarios that he might encounter, the situations and the individuals that will need to be controlled throughout. On the way out of the house to leave for the game, he would always make the same promise to his family: 'Everything will be fine.' Then he would drive to a Glasgow city-centre hotel, to meet with his assistants and eat a meal (breakfast for Old Firm games, as the kick-offs are now always midday or 12.30 p.m., to prevent supporters being able to drink heavily beforehand).

The schedule is the same for every match, but the atmosphere is different on the mornings of Old Firm encounters; there is less small talk, faces tend to be grave and solemn as the officials run through the procedures of the game and how the referee will communicate with his assistants, what signals to look out for. They arrive at the stadium at least ninety minutes before kick-off. Already, there are more police, more media, more supporters milling around than for any other game; an atmosphere already exists, something heavy and forbidding, as though they are all at the mercy of this game. Everybody is on edge; everything is heightened. The attitude around them is different, people are uptight, exchanging glances that are wary, preoc-cupied. The referee heads straight into the officials' dressing room. Police officers arrive to do their briefing about security and any intel-ligence they may have about planned disturbances, as well as how many officers will escort the officials off the field and up the tunnel at the end of the game. Most of it passes the referee and his assistants by; they are engrossed in their own fate, the relationship between the match, this often belligerent confrontation, and their decisions.

The referee then visits the home and away team dressing rooms, to remind the players of their obligations: 'No aggressive behaviour,' he says to them. 'Respect each other and the officials, no dangerous play. If you go into the crowd, you're going to be cautioned. Realise the atmosphere you're in, don't be giving any gestures to the opposing fans, cupping the ear, all that kind of stuff. It's different today, lads.' The mood of each dressing room is revealing: if music is blaring and the players are boisterous, the team is likely to be animated. Every signal has to be recognised and understood. A brooding dressing room tells of a side that is about to be overwhelmed, and every match official is most alarmed by the prospect of a one-sided game, as the beaten team will often then lose their self-control.

Before kick-off, Dallas would sit in the referee's toilet with the team sheets, working out in his mind how the players will line up and where he will find the ones he considers antsy and most likely to over-react – those who need to be managed by him more urgently than others. Then there would be final instructions to his assistants.

'Just give what you see, not what you hear from the crowd,' he says. 'And remember, look at me, to see my decisions, because you won't hear my whistle. Not out there. Not in this game.'

Normally, when the players gather in the tunnel before kick-off, they talk to each other, either warmly or in gently mocking tones. At an Old Firm game, they stand in silence, almost like a vigil. Dallas would often pick out one player with a fierce reputation as he walked up between the two teams, carrying the match ball under his arm, or one who had made comments about the other team during the build-up, and loudly warn him: 'I'm well aware of what's going on here today. I read the paper yesterday, I know what you said.' Then he stands at the front of the two teams, looking down to the end of the tunnel, where the walls narrow to reveal a patch of green. The grass looks peaceful, unblemished, although a noise can be heard. Before he begins to walk out – when nothing can be undone, only endured – the referee stands, aware of the players lining up behind him, their occasional movements, the presence of a spreading agitation. Once the ball boys are outside, the noise gathers at the edge of the tunnel, sharp and angry, and as the referee walks down towards the pitch, leading everybody out, there is one thought uppermost in his mind: 'I must get the first decision right. Everything rides on it. Control, authority, be stern. Be right.'

Outside, it is vicious, the noise is frenzied, so that even thoughts are drowned out. Everybody is suddenly exposed, eleven players on either side, two assistants on either touchline, and one referee, in the middle, essentially alone. The adrenalin is up, the heart rate has risen sharply, the senses are acute. Already, the referee is watching how the captains interact – warmly, indifferently, antagonistically – what the other players are doing, the coaching staff, the supporters all around. The uproar is powerful, and the referee has to be aware of it all, as if his gaze must be everywhere at once, seeing everything. But, in turn, everybody is watching him.

'You're under a lot more scrutiny,' Dallas says. 'If you give a wrong decision, then in the west of Scotland there's got to be a reason why you did that, you went to this school or that school. I've never been brought up in that community, that sectarianism, that bias. When you get that, you wonder, "Why is my credibility getting called into question here, it's just a game of football." But it's much more than that. You feel isolated. I can remember giving a penalty kick to Celtic at Ibrox, at the opposite end from the Celtic end, when John Hartson went down under a challenge from Lorenzo Amoruso. There was no claim or roar for it; if you start thinking of consequences, you should never be in that position. It's after it you think, "I hope I've got that right." As you're heading into your position, you're aware that the replays from all different angles are being shown all over the world and you're just praying that you got it right and it's showing what you've seen. That's the other thing that's different, if you go to do Hearts v. Celtic, there's eight cameras at the game, for Rangers v. Celtic it's twenty-four. You're aware that there's no hiding place; you've just got to get the decisions right.'

'Offside. No. 10, Fortune, flag's up. Free kick.' The noise, the booing, it's savage, for an offside decision. I hope that call was right, another close one. It must have been right. 'Take the free kick from there, where you are. Come on, hurry up.' How long have we played? Twenty-one minutes, is that all? Bloody hell. Both watches still working. Cards, notebook, pencil, whistle. What next?

'Foul.' Another free kick, Rangers No. 5, Sasa Papac, on Celtic No. 19, Barry Robson. 'Sasa, no more, that was a clear foul. Another and you'll be in the book.' Right, where are we? 'Take it from there, don't move the ball.' What's happening on the bench, who's the fourth official speaking to? Why? This noise, it's

incessant. 'Offside, Celtic No. 22, Glenn Loovens. Free kick. Take
it from there, Allan. There. Move it back.' Another foul. Rangers
No. 2, Maurice Edu, and No. 21, Kirk Broadfoot, on Celtic No.
6, Landry N'Guemo. 'Free kick.' Fortune's through. No. 'Offside,
flag's up, free kick.' Twenty-six minutes gone. It's bedlam. What
next?

Foul. Rangers No. 27, Kyle Lafferty, on Celtic No. 2, Andreas
Hinkel. That's a bad one, he caught him late. Were the studs up?
'Are you okay, Andreas? Physio, come on.' How bad was it? It
looked bad. The fans reacted. Red or yellow? Red or yellow? Yellow,
I'm certain. 'Come here.' I've warned him already. That's a foul,
you can't lunge in like that. 'Number? Yellow card.' Rangers No.
27, Kyle Lafferty, foul tackle on Celtic No. 2, Andreas Hinkel, thirty
minutes. That's another one, they're all watching it again already.
How bad was it? I called it as I saw it. Was it worse? Hinkel
seemed badly hurt. They all know. All of them. I hope I got it
right. I must have got it right. Both watches still working. Cards,
notebook, pencil, whistle. What next?

Jim Duncan took charge of his first, and only, Old Firm match at
Ibrox in October 1987. He knew something of what to expect, as
every official in Scotland does, but the full magnitude of each Rangers
v. Celtic encounter cannot be predicted. There was a vindictiveness
around Ibrox; Rangers were in the second season of Graeme Souness's
management (in which conceit, ambition and money combined to
radically transform not only the club but the very nature of Scottish
football), while Celtic, under Billy McNeill, were months away from
the start of their centenary year, a time that the club wanted to mark
with success, and a reassertion of superiority over Rangers, something
they were almost desperate to achieve.

It was also Frank McAvennie's first Old Firm game, the Celtic striker having returned to Glasgow following a prolific and glitzy spell in London with West Ham. He had long blond hair and a mischievous grin, with a nascent celebrity and a reputation for glamour and women; you looked at McAvennie and saw the sharp edges of a different kind of stardom, something glaring and soulless that was beginning to seep into football. And on his Old Firm debut, he stuck to a familiar habit on the pitch.

At the first opportunity, McAvennie hurled himself at Chris Woods, as the Rangers goalkeeper jumped to claim a high ball, knowing that he would not be booked so early in the game, but also that a little doubt would then be left in the goalkeeper's mind when the next cross came in. The barge, which sent Woods into the goal after he had tipped the ball over, was left unpunished by Duncan, who did not see the infringement and so awarded a corner instead of a free kick. The Rangers defenders – among them the bluntly imposing and brawny Terry Butcher, and the sly, brutal Graham Roberts – were furious, while the Celtic fans, sitting right behind the goal, were in uproar.

Minutes later, when another cross was driven into the Rangers penalty area, Woods moved to collect the ball. But McAvennie also charged towards the goalkeeper, who raised his left arm, stiff and horizontal, to meet the challenge. The Celtic striker then clipped Woods round the side of the head with a callous flick of his left hand and both players reacted aggressively, prompting Butcher to lumber over and roughly shove McAvennie with both hands. Roberts also came across, with his arms raised, and McAvennie fell to the ground clutching his face. Ibrox, from all sides, reacted with a terrible fury, and after seventeen minutes of the game Duncan found himself in the midst of turmoil. He called Woods and McAvennie across and, clutching his notebook and cards, lectured them. He was smaller than the two players and they looked down on him, in his black uniform, as wisps of his hair were blown upright in the wind. After motioning that McAvennie had thrown a punch, Duncan raised the red card to the Celtic striker, who walked off looking aghast, then did the same for Woods, who pulled off his goalkeeper's jersey and handed it to Roberts, before jogging off, his muscled torso pale in the shadow cast by the Ibrox main stand. An enraged Butcher was also booked.

An edge revealed itself in the aftermath, something spiteful. Celtic took the lead through their striker Andy Walker, then Butcher, under pressure from Celtic midfielder Peter Grant, diverted the ball over Roberts' head to make the score 2–0. Grant then ran to the Celtic support, slid onto his knees, blessed himself by making the sign of the cross on his chest with his right hand, then raised both arms skyward. It was an impulsive act, and one that the midfielder – whose Catholic faith has always been a significant and cherished part of his life – later deeply regretted (although the majority of Rangers fans could not have been certain of seeing it, and much of the furore arose after it had been shown in the television coverage of the game; days later, Grant was sent a copy of the Italian newspaper *Corriere dello Sport* that carried a picture of him on his knees under the headline 'Il Cattolico' in its centre pages).

After the interval, Butcher was involved in another flashpoint. He leapt to challenge Allen McKnight, the Celtic goalkeeper, in the penalty area, and their legs tangled as they fell. Butcher then seemed to push McKnight back to the ground, who rolled over with his hands to his face, and Duncan sent the Rangers captain off. The game finished 2–2, with Ally McCoist scoring soon after Butcher's dismissal, then Richard Gough scrambling an equaliser in the last minute. There was still time for Roberts to feign injury after being bumped into by Owen Archdeacon, the Celtic winger, and stand with one foot on the ball while wafting his arms in the air, as if conducting the Rangers fans while they sang:

> Hello, hello,
> We are the Billy Boys;
> Hello, hello,
> You'll know us by our noise;
> We're up to our knees in Fenian blood;
> Surrender or you'll die;
> For we are the Brigton Derry Boys

The aftermath of the game was torrid, as outrage enveloped Duncan, the players and the two clubs. David Holmes, the Rangers chairman, and Jack McGinn, his Celtic counterpart, met to discuss the events and the outcry, then Sandy Jessop, the Procurator Fiscal, intervened, having watched footage of the incidents with the solicitor-general for Scotland, the lord advocate and two advocates-depute. On 1 November, Woods, Butcher, Roberts and McAvennie were summoned to Govan police station and charged with 'conduct likely to provoke a breach of the peace among spectators'. Rangers and Celtic appointed Len Murray, one of Scotland's leading solicitors, to defend the players. On 20 November, the charge was altered to 'while participating in a football match, you did conduct yourself in a disorderly manner and commit a breach of the peace'.

On 12 April 1988, the trial began, and among the witnesses was the Assistant Chief Constable of Strathclyde, John Dickson, who claimed that he had feared a pitch invasion at Ibrox: 'There was unbridled hatred on the faces of some of the fans when they were shouting obscenities and insults at each other.' Duncan was also called as a witness, and told the court, after the incident was replayed on a television screen, that he had responded to what he saw on the pitch at the time, not the replays, and that he had not seen Roberts' involvement in the initial altercation, or his conducting of the Rangers fans' songs at the end of the game.

As he passed sentence, Sheriff Archibald McKay said to Woods that the video evidence 'clearly established that you jabbed McAvennie on the chin with your left forearm. It was an assault which constituted breach of the peace'. McKay told Butcher that he was guilty of a 'violent push . . . which might reasonably have been expected to upset other Celtic players and their support'. Then to all four defendants he added: 'A large percentage of supporters are readily converted by breaches of the peace into two rival mobs. That they were not so transformed is no credit to you. You must have been aware of your wider responsibilities and you failed to discharge them.' Woods was found guilty and fined £500, Butcher guilty and fined £250, while Roberts was found not proven and McAvennie not guilty.

Duncan worked as a grade one referee for a further four years, but never in another Old Firm game, then quit the profession, having lost his enthusiasm for being a match official. 'It's win at all cost,' he later said about clashes between Celtic and Rangers. 'Both sets of fans have blinkers on and don't see the ref until a decision goes against them, then it's his fault for their team losing the game. It was a baptism of fire for me. Fans don't realise refs can't see everything. As a referee you can't have eyes in the back of your head.'

Foul. 'Free kick.' Rangers No. 9, Kris Boyd, on Celtic No. 17, Marc Crosas. 'Take the kick.' Another foul. 'Free kick.' Rangers No. 3, David Weir, on Celtic No. 9, Georgios Samaras. 'Walk away, David. Walk away. Right, that's it, come here. That was a foul. Stop yelling in my face. Don't question my authority. Walk.' How long until half time? Thirteen minutes. Both watches still working. Cards, notebook, pencil, whistle. What next?

Rangers have changed formation here, one up front I think.

*They're steeling themselves, Celtic have had most of the game.
Rangers will be digging in now, defending, I'll need to watch for
aggression or professional fouls. This game is in the balance.
'Corner. From the left. Wait for the whistle.' What's happening in
the box now? Keep watching. Forty-four minutes gone. One substitution. I'll add on two minutes for injury time, then it's the
interval. I need that break. What now? Nothing. This noise never
lets up.*

*Both watches still working. Cards, notebook, pencil, whistle.
What next? Police and stewards are out, how long to go? Thirty
seconds. What's happening over there? Just a tussle. Not long to
go. Not long. Right, half time. That's it. Whistle. 'I'll take the ball,
please. Thank you.' Where is my assistant? OK? Anything
happening on the pitch? The stands? Are the players all off? Where
are the police? Right, up the tunnel. Sanctuary.*

The dressing room is silent at first, a stark contrast from the bedlam
the match officials have just left behind. There is no television,
just refreshments and a muted, almost stunned air. Some referees
ask a colleague or friend to text them at half time during televised
games, to let them know if they have called the contentious
decisions right. Dallas tries to discourage this, as knowing or
believing that he has made an error can affect a referee's mindset.
He always gives match officials the same piece of advice that he
received early in his career: 'If you realise you've made a mistake
in the game, don't try to even it up, because then you've doubled
your mistakes.'

It is an opportunity for respite, to try to regain that feeling of
being controlled, shrewd, sharp-witted, at a time when the senses
are still frantic. Dallas has attended many of the game's major derby

matches, including AC Milan v. Internazionale, Real Madrid v. Barcelona, and Uruguay v. Brazil in Montevideo, but only one game has come close to the sheer frenzy – of emotion, of intensity, of drama, of pressure – that is the central characteristic of the Old Firm fixture: Galatasaray v. Fenerbahce, in Istanbul. 'I went in to see the referee after the game and I could understand what he was going through,' Dallas says. 'He was just sitting there, as if he'd been in a barrel with ten guys hitting it with shovels. He was stunned, shocked.'

During the half-time interval, the assistant referees exchange information about the attacking and defending tactics of the two teams, and personal quirks of the players – who runs offside before running back on, who steps up quickly or slowly, or plays on the shoulder of the last man and times his runs on the edge of being offside – since they are swapping teams in the second half. Then all the cautions are checked, and the referee reminds his assistants again to watch him rather than listen for his whistle and to be strong, to make decisions with authority and confidence. Dallas used to walk round the dressing room, keeping on the move so that his muscles did not seize up. Once the calm has descended, it feels unnerving and the impulse is to go back outside again, to revive that feeling of urgent concentration.

'I know Pierluigi Collina would have swapped any derby to have an Old Firm game on his CV,' Dallas says. 'I wouldn't have swapped it to have a Milan derby. Old Firm games are special and they're the one thing that you miss when you retire. You need to be in the city, living in it. The English guys talk about the Manchester derby, but it can be refereed by someone from London, so he comes in, does the game and goes home that night, which is great for him, but you don't really understand what it's all about. Pierre van Hooijdonk scored an equalising goal in a 3–3 game that I did [at Ibrox], and I'd already cautioned him. He ran into the crowd to celebrate and I was under strict instructions to issue a caution for that. I was quite inexperienced at the time, but I can remember him running into the goal, then into the crowd, and the place was in uproar. I thought, "If I put this guy off here, there will be mayhem." I can always remember that Campbell Ogilvie [the Rangers club secretary] came into the dressing room with the police afterwards to say, "Thanks very much for not putting Van Hooijdonk off, because there would have been havoc here." It's just that split-second decision. I kicked Van Hooijdonk's arse all the way back to the halfway line and told him in no uncertain terms, "You sneeze from now to the end of the game and you're up that tunnel." He realised. That's the common sense that you've got to use in games like that.'

Nobody is allowed near the referee's dressing room at half time, as emotions are already high and the match officials are the natural target for any discontent. Often, a police officer will stand outside the door, to be sure that nobody tries to gain access in the heat of the moment. At Celtic Park, the dressing room opens into a hallway that leads from the hospitality suites to the seats in the main stand. So the officials leave early, to make sure they do not encounter any supporters returning outside.

Watches, both of them, working. Cards, red and yellow, back pocket, top pocket. Notebook, pencil, coin. Whistle. Check my watch, 1.30 p.m. Eleven players on both sides. Assistants in place. Where's the signal from the television official? Okay. Okay. Here we go. Again.

Foul. 'Free kick, Celtic. Yes, Kris, foul. Walk away.' Rangers No. 9, Kris Boyd, on Celtic No. 5, Gary Caldwell. Thirty-one seconds. Is that all it takes? There's no let-up. It just goes on and on. Rangers are still digging in, it's all Celtic. One side dominating. I'll need to keep a heavy hand on this.

That's McGeady through, no flag, onside. He's missed it. 'Goal kick.' That was a chance. 'Come on, Allan, take the kick. No time-wasting.' McGeady again. Over the bar. 'Goal kick.' Another chance. Foul. 'Free kick.' Celtic No. 17, Marc Crosas, on Rangers No. 2, Maurice Edu. Another foul. 'Free kick. Come here. Here. Look, you've been warned, that's yet another foul. You're in the book. Number? Right, any more of that and you'll be off.' Rangers No. 9, Kris Boyd, booked for foul play, challenge on Celtic No. 11, Danny Fox, fifty-three minutes.

Both watches still working. Cards, notebook, pencil, whistle. What next? Foul. 'Free kick. Come here. That's a booking, no arguing, you brought him down. Stop it. Number? Yellow card.' Booking, Rangers No. 16, Steven Whittaker, tackle on Celtic No. 17, Marc Crosas, sixty-two minutes played. Okay, keep going, keep asserting yourself, stay in control. Boyd's through. No. Flag's up. 'Offside. Yes you were, Kris, the flag is up. Free kick, from there. Wait for the whistle.' What now, what's that signal? Substitute. 'Okay, make the change.' Celtic No. 17, off, No. 7 on. Scott McDonald, that's a bold change. Celtic will be going for it now, the pressure will be on Rangers and their defenders. I'll need to watch them and McDonald.

Foul. 'Free kick. That was deliberate, you're in the book. Number? Yellow card.' Rangers No. 3, David Weir, unsporting behaviour, foul on Celtic No. 10, Marc-Antoine Fortune, seventy-two minutes. Something's got to give here, it's incessant. 'Corner. From the right. Wait for the whistle.' Watch the penalty area, what's happening in there? In it comes, McDonald shot, blocked. What next? McGeady, cross. 'Goal.' Is the flag up? No. Goal. Celtic No. 7, Scott McDonald, seventy-eight minutes, 1–0. Where's he celebrating. 'On the pitch, Scott, stay on the pitch.' My God, the noise, the movement, what is happening? There's too much going on. This place has erupted. 'Away from the fans, don't leave the field of play. Back now, back.'

Both watches still working. Cards, notebook, pencil, whistle. What next? 'Kick-off.' This can go two ways now – Rangers will react positively, or lose the place. I've got to keep an eye on every-thing. Ball's out of play on the right. 'Corner. Wait for the whistle.' What's happening in the box? Watch them. Who's that shoving? Watch them. Over it comes. 'Goal.' Rangers No. 6, Lee McCulloch, eighty minutes, 1–1. 'Away from the fans, don't leave the field of play, Lee. Back. Back.'

On the morning of Sunday, 2 May 1999, Dallas went to his local gym for a swim, then took a stroll round Strathclyde Park with his wife, Jackie. It was a hot summer's day, the sunlight was glinting and the air was thick with that languor of a bank holiday weekend. As they drove home around midday, up through Motherwell, Dallas noticed Old Firm supporters out in numbers, drinking on grass verges and outside pubs. The kick-off was 6 p.m. in the evening. As Dallas drove through the village where he lives, he passed several bars where Celtic fans congregate, and more people were sitting outside, drinking. In his car, Dallas thought to himself: 'Jesus Christ.'

When he arrived at Celtic Park, around four o'clock in the after-noon, a hostility was already evident, something malign. Celtic offi-cials were anxious about the event, with a Rangers victory enough to secure the Championship, which would be the first time the Ibrox side had achieved that feat at the home of their fierce rivals. And that significance, combined with the late kick-off and the following day being a bank holiday, caused a sense of alarm. Even during the warm-up, Dallas felt uneasy. The stadium was fuller than usual for so long before kick-off, and the atmosphere was already fraught. The Rangers fans were celebrating (their side was ten points ahead and all but assured of winning the title) and the Celtic support was seething. By the time he stood in the narrow tunnel, with the teams lining up behind him, Dallas was certain that the match would be volatile and difficult to control.

The opening exchanges of the game were frantic. Dallas asserted his authority by being strict, and booked Stephane Mahe, Celtic's French defender, after he furiously confronted the referee in a glaring show of dissent, claiming that Paul Lambert, the Celtic midfielder, had been elbowed by Rod Wallace, the Rangers striker. Mahe was almost manic in his behaviour – his wildly staring eyes, his hollow features and unruly hair accentuating his apparent lack of self-control – and Dallas spoke to Tom Boyd, the Celtic captain, telling him to calm the player down. But when Mahe reacted angrily to a heavy challenge by Neil McCann, the Rangers winger, in the thirtieth minute and gesticulated wildly that the player should be booked, Dallas showed him a second yellow card. The Frenchman lost his temper, running up to the referee and shouting aggressively, then lunging towards him before teammates struggled to restrain him. The Frenchman then had to be ushered forcibly from the field.

The incident seemed to epitomise the mood of the day – unhinged, fearful – and incited antagonism among the Celtic players and fans. Twelve minutes later, Dallas awarded a free kick to Rangers (who were already 1–0 up through a McCann goal) near the corner flag at Celtic's end of the pitch. There was confusion about whether it was a free kick or a corner, and Dallas jogged over to hurry along Giovanni van Bronckhorst, the Rangers midfielder – which he did by telling the Dutch midfielder to 'Get your arse over there and take the free kick', then patting him on the backside, as Dallas was always a tactile referee. Then a Celtic fan ran onto the pitch and straight towards Dallas, only to be stopped by players and stewards.

As the game was about to restart, a fifty pence coin thrown from among the Celtic fans hit Dallas on the forehead, and when he raised his fingertips to the source of the ache, he saw blood.

'I felt this thud and thought, "What was that?", then I could feel the blood,' he says. 'Brian Scott [the Celtic physio] and the Celtic doctor came on and said I had to go off. But I said, "There's no way I'm coming off, trust me, get Vaseline on it. There are only two minutes to half time, I'm not coming off." In any other country in Europe, the game would have been abandoned, that's what referees are told, but I can imagine Strathclyde's finest if I'd abandoned that game and they've got 60,000 people spilling onto the streets. I'd been hit by coins before, all referees have, they ping off your shoulder, but that one just hit the target.'

The atmosphere was so belligerent that some of the Celtic substitutes warming up behind the goal were fearful, and jogged back to the dugout. When Van Bronckhorst took the free kick, Dallas saw a foul in the penalty area and awarded a spot kick to Rangers. Once the consternation of the players had subsided, another fan ran onto the pitch towards Dallas, only to be restrained under a pile of yellow-jacketed stewards.

At half time, while the Celtic ground staff gathered up objects that had been thrown onto the pitch during the first forty-five minutes, Dallas received four stitches in his head wound and a pain-killing injection. He then phoned his wife, Jackie, who was watching the game at home on television. 'I'm fine, I'm fine,' he said, trying to calm her fears. 'It was just a coin.'

By the end of the game, Dallas had sent off two more players – Wallace and Vidar Riseth, Celtic's Norwegian defender – while a Celtic supporter had fallen from an upper tier of one stand onto the crowd below. When he was eventually carried away on a stretcher, he raised his arm in triumph. The game finished 3–0 to Rangers, and the players briefly gathered in a huddle during the celebrations in front of their own fans, an act calculated to mock the huddle that Celtic players engage in before every game. Afterwards, stewards lifted a total of £78 worth of coins from the pitch.

As always, Dallas left Celtic Park swiftly with his team of officials, returning to the city-centre hotel where they had left their cars, then driving on to his Lanarkshire home. Later on, while Dallas was in the sitting room at the back of his house with Jackie and Andrew, one of the couple's two sons, he heard glass smashing round the front. When he ran out to the garden, Dallas found two beer bottles on the ground and the outer panes of two of his double-glazed windows smashed. Police later arrested the culprit – a double-glazing executive, Kevin Dunn – who turned out to be a near neighbour who had been drinking. Nobody was hurt, but the incident further intensified the indignation that grew in Scottish society following the scenes at the game, which had been broadcast live across the UK and beyond.

'Supporters know where you live,' says Dallas, who himself owned a double-glazing firm. 'I live between two villages which have big Celtic followings. It was quite surreal, because I got up the next morning and went to work, just because I had an appointment. It was a bank holiday on the Monday, but I had to go into the office up in Perth that day. I went to my work for nine o'clock, fine, then Jackie phoned to say, "Hugh the place is crawling with media guys." I said, "Tell them I'm in Perth", but they weren't having it, so they waited. I had the Old Firm cup final three weeks later, which I was revelling in, I couldn't wait for it to come along.'

Between the two Old Firm games, Dallas's house was put under police protection, with an unmarked car patrolling the area and maintaining surveillance on the property itself. When the referee attended the opening of Hampden's new South Stand days later, he was accompanied by four bodyguards.

'The reason that it's different is because living in the west of Scotland makes a difference, you're right in the middle of it,' Dallas says.

'We in Scotland just live in a village, everybody knows what's going on. It affects your business. You go into the business community and you're dealing with Rangers and Celtic fans, and it definitely affected my business contacts. People you would be in contact with prior to a game wouldn't speak to me for maybe two or three years afterwards. It's extremely unprofessional in the business world, but it did go on. I could name major building companies who would not deal with me because of the Old Firm thing. You've just got to learn to cope with that and be the bigger person.'

Nine minutes left to play. What next? Foul. 'Free kick.' Rangers No. 21, Kirk Broadfoot, on Celtic No. 9, Georgios Samaras. It's going to be a hectic finish. What's left to happen in this game? It could be anything. I hope I called all the big decisions right: that Fortune header, that Lafferty tackle, they're the ones, that's what people will be talking about. I'm sure I got them right, I must have done. I hope so. Not long to go now. Both watches still working. Cards, notebook, pencil, whistle. What next?

Foul. 'Free kick.' Rangers No. 16, Steven Whittaker, on Celtic No. 19, Barry Robson. Celtic will go all out here, they need to win. There might be something left in this yet, I have to stay in charge. Focus. Wait, what's that? Weir and McDonald. 'Stop that, you two. I won't have any of that. No confrontations. Scott, over there. David, that way. Walk away. Both of you, walk away. Leave it.' Still it goes on, this frenzy, I've never known anything like it.

How long to go? Two minutes. Okay. Only one substitution. I'll add on two minutes. That's all. Nearly there. What next? Corner to Celtic. 'Wait for the whistle.' Watch what's happening in the penalty area. Keep watching. A goal now would cause pandemonium. Overhead kick. Loovens. Wide. Both watches still working. Cards, notebook, pencil, whistle. What next? Almost there. Almost. Assistants, check. We're beyond two minutes. When this ball is in the air . . . That's it. Whistle. 'Full time.' Shake hands. It's over. My God, it's over.

When the final whistle blows, the stand-side assistant referee immediately heads up the tunnel to try to prevent flare-ups between the players as they return to the dressing rooms. The referee, carrying the match ball, and his other assistant are the last to leave the pitch, with an escort of stewards and police. An officer will stand again outside the referee's dressing room, to prevent any players, coaches or club officials trying to make a point about something contentious that happened in the game. Mostly, though, everybody involved is mentally and physically drained. A sudden fatigue overcomes the referee and his assistants, even though their minds continues to be a clutter of anxieties and recollections.

Back in the dressing room, the officials run through, again, the bookings and other incidents that will be included in the referee's report. But the process is quick, as the urge now is to go home, to leave behind the furore. And there is always the worry that something has been called wrong, that one decision more than any other is now the focus of the game, is being pored over by supporters and players and journalists. Those decisions run through the referee's head, clear in detail but vague at the moment of contention. Was it the right call to only yellow-card Lafferty? What about Fortune's goal, was it right to disallow it? The match official, as always, will become the scapegoat. It is time to go, to take refuge.

The referee heads home and, whatever the outcome of the game, considers whether it is better to stay in, or go out for dinner to a discreet and private restaurant, somewhere familiar, where they are known and guaranteed space in which to be undisturbed, concealed almost. There are plenty of times when the profile of the job brings welcome recognition, but heading into the city or town centre on the night of the game could turn out to be a form of incitement.

'I can honestly tell you that with one exception, in all the times that I was out, I was never abused,' says Dallas. 'It's probably now that I've retired that people will say things like that, because they know you've stopped refereeing. Whether they thought it could affect their team when I was refereeing was part of it, I don't know. In the city centre, I'd go to restaurants and it would be very positive, people would come over and want pictures taking with you and autographs. Only once, at a Scotland game, was there a guy who had a right go at me. My wife was with me. He was a St Johnstone fan, and this guy had been drinking. The police whisked him away. This was five minutes before the national anthem, so he never even saw the game. But that's the only time that's happened.'

What fills the public consciousness for the days that follow depends on the incidents of the game. If there was something controversial, something that one of the teams can claim affected the outcome in the other side's favour, then the performance of the referee is agonised over. Fortune's disallowed goal, Lafferty's tackle on Hinkel – they are debated endlessly, in newspapers, on the radio, on the internet, everywhere that supporters gather. So Conroy becomes the story: who is he, where does he come from, what's his background, what team does he support, what school did he go to, Catholic or Protestant? Green or blue?

Naturally, the referee reads all the newspapers the following day, to see how much of a target he has become, or to see if his performance has been praised. He knows himself which areas of the game he performed well at and what he did wrong, but he pores over the papers because the fans read them, and because he needs to know what the news cycle will be, if his performance is to become a self-perpetuating drama.

'It can go longer than a week,' Dallas says. 'If it goes positively, you're quite keen to go to work on the Monday and bump into people. You know that the television people have been quite complimentary about you, the newspapers have been complimentary about you, and so you're walking tall. But there are days, Blunder Ref, Hugh Plonker, when you think, "Oh my God", and you stay low key. But you've got to go out and face it, you've put yourself in that position as a football referee. The rewards are great and you accept that you're going to have bad days.'

CHAPTER 3
IN THE STANDS

You gather in the streets around the ground, watching and listening, mostly to each other, but also for their fans, and the police. People mingle between parked cars or in doorways, in groups of three or four, muttering and looking around. You open another beer, and toss the bottle cap up the close, and it clatters on the stone steps. That's the last of the carry-out now, and already you can sense the spirit of the day from the fans around you. There are a few grim faces, but also knowing grins. 'You up for this the day, son? Get that down yer neck, eh.' There is a tightness in your stomach, and the awareness of a steady but still intermittent movement of people in one direction, towards the stadium. A police car drives by at the end of the road, and you turn your back on them so they can't see you drinking, but most of the others don't bother. Then someone throws an empty bottle across the street towards an old embankment. It bounces off the railings and smashes on the ground. He looks at it, and shrugs. 'Fuck it.' And everything feels edgy, there is a taut atmosphere; you want to be on the move. 'Shall we go?'

Your friends have finished their beers, and you down the last of your own, then begin the walk towards Celtic Park across the uneven pavement, where weeds grow up between cracks, and dodging between the discarded cans and bottles. The five of you walk to the end of the road, and join a larger group as you turn the corner. The pace is quicker, more urgent, and it feels good to be among them, all of you wearing the same colour of scarves, belonging with each other. The more people who join the throng, the closer together you all become. Then a chant starts up ahead that ripples all the way back to the end of what must now be thirty-odd people. You don't know the man walking directly beside you, but he smiles pensively and you respond in the same way.

As you approach the ground, there are police and stewards everywhere, watching and listening intently. You glance at the ground and run your fingers along the outline of the hip flask tucked into the waistband of your trousers, then check your inside jacket pocket. The ticket is still there. By now, you just want to be inside the ground, and part of the game. You can still taste that last swig of beer – sharp and warm – and feel a little light-headed. But it's a pleasant sensation as you're carried along by the momentum of the crowd. These are your people, this is your team, you have a part to play. Nothing else matters now but being here. You want to join the turnstile queue immediately, because the fear is that your line will be the slow one and you'll be left outside waiting when the game kicks off. Anxiety rises as you walk past the stewards, who seem grim and downcast in their luminous jackets, a lugubrious roundness to their watching faces, and the stern presence of the police, their frowning, squinting eyes and that sense of arch superiority, then into the turnstile itself. What if the ticket is fake? What if I hold everybody up here? What if I have to leave on my own now? Then into the twisting metal gates that seem to trap you for an instant in a cold steel cage, pressing against your legs, your arms, your back, as you are herded inside with a slow, grating clank.

You check the ticket for the area of your seat, then cast an eye around the direction signs, but you're still only aware of a movement of people, a steady push through the concourse. The concrete floors are solid and seem grainy underfoot, and all the metalwork is green – chipped in places, but an enduring, earnest green – and then up the stairs, flight after flight, marching, before heading outside. The doorways are narrow, with room enough only for two people side by side, and everybody is wrapped up for the cold weather in big, thick jackets, hats and boots. Somebody slaps you on the back: 'Here we go, let's give it to 'em, those bastards. Here we fuckin' go.' The light catches you first, so bright that it seems to carry a sharp edge, then the growing noise, something alive and vigorous. You feel indispensable, and when you take your seat, alongside your friends and fellow supporters, surrounded on all sides, you are utterly lost to the occasion. And it seems that nothing else exists except for here and now.

'You feel like you're part of the Rangers representative army and I'm sure it's the same for Celtic fans,' says David Edgar, a Rangers supporter. 'Nobody enjoys going to Old Firm games. You don't wake up and you're desperate to go, it's a really strange, queasy sensation. Me, I'm up at five o'clock, can't sleep, bouncing out of bed. I've given up the drink, but in the old days there would be a social club open from about eight o'clock, or there would be somebody's house, so the drink would be flowing early. I know loads of guys who get hammered on a Saturday night and turn up after pulling an all-nighter. You can't sleep, you try to force some food down, the heart's beating, your hands are shaking, you're twitchy, you're nervous, you're talking out your arse. You're talking bravado, you're bantering with your friends. It's very much a friend thing, you all get together before it. I don't know anybody who would just turn at the game on their own. It's part of that comradeship thing. You go through your pre-match rituals, which are far worse that day than any other – I don't wear that jacket to the game, or I wore that aftershave once and we won. You go through everything and you really become a poster boy for OCD, anything to deflect your mind from it.

'At the game, you're very much segregated from the other fans, so you get a real feeling of, "this is where Rangers fans go, you're in with your people, your fellow supporters". You've got to park the car or supporters' bus in a certain area, you're herded into a certain area. For a fan attending an away Old Firm match, it's as much about how you perform as the team. You feel the weight of responsibility that you've got to out-sing the home fans, make sure the players know they've got a hundred per cent backing. There's a sort of military aspect to it, you feel like part of an invading army and you know you're up against a significantly bigger force, but you know you're going to box clever. There's a lot more humour in the away support. You really do feel part of something special, more so at Parkhead or an away European game. There's a real togetherness. You're enclosed in one area, you're all locked in together and a bond forms in that time.'

Once in place, the songs begin. On one side:

> For it's a grand old team to play for
> For it's a grand old team to see
> And if you know your history
> It's enough to make your heart go whoa-oh
> We don't care what the animals say
> What the hell do we care
> For we only know that there's gonna be a show
> And the Glasgow Celtic will be there

And from the other side of the stadium, as if in direct response, as though the singing duties are to be shared and competed over:

It is old but it is beautiful
It's colours they are fine
It was worn at Derry, Aughrim, Enniskillen
And the Boyne
My father wore it as a youth
In bygone days of yore
So on the Twelfth I proudly wear
The sash my father wore
Fuck the Pope.

Even the individual voices become assimilated. Few people eat, because pies, Bovril or the other routines of a match day are a distraction, and everybody is too tense. There is little talk about the game, as it is too noisy to be heard properly, but there are mutterings and exclamations about which players have made the starting line-up and which have been left out. When the team's warm-up carries the players across the pitch towards the fans, a spontaneous cheer is released towards the players, as though every exhortation could be transformed into an extra ounce of determination. When the opposition team is read out over the Tannoy, each name is jeered where you are and cheered elsewhere; and when your team is read out, the opposite occurs.

It is ritualistic, this ceremony, part of a theatrical sense of occasion. At an Old Firm game, the supporters are engaged in a contest as much as the players; the fans spar with each other, provoking and retaliating, so that the match itself is at times irrelevant. What is being asserted are two identities: Rangers and Celtic. There are other boundaries: Protestant and Catholic/Unionist and Republican/ Conservative and Socialist/the south of Glasgow and the east of Glasgow, but they can be shared among the two sets of fans; whatever the personal distinction, and no matter how insignificant it might be, the purpose is for one club's followers to dominate the other, to emphatically be its superior.

'Without question, it's reassuring to know that there's a camara-derie between your fellow supporters,' says Gerry McDade, a Celtic fan. 'They feel as you feel . . . they worry the way you do. You know that the toilet paper sales in their houses are as exactly increased as yours are in the days running up to the match. Inside the stadium, the atmosphere is different. Firstly, there's a defiance from the Celtic support. This is our lair . . . you may have slipped in to watch the festivities, but you must listen to our PA, our renditions of the Willy Maley Song, The Celtic Song and, of course, "You'll Never Walk Alone". We are tense, the guts are churning, and then there's that almighty roar as the teams come out onto the pitch.'

At pre-arranged signals, you walk down the aisle you are covering, as your fellow stewards do the same around the ground, looking from one side to the other at the supporters, and then waiting, either crouched at the bottom of the stairs, or at the top, near an entrance or a wall, for the next signal. You are always watching, and being watched, responding to the fans as they engage with each other or the events on the pitch. In your high-viz jacket you feel exposed, but being among the fans means you've avoided the duties that nobody wants – being stuck outside the stadium while the game is being played, doing the ticket checks or manning the dividing lines between the two sets of supporters. There are 300 stewards, much more than for a normal game, and the instructions have been terse: 'If you catch someone smoking, drinking or doing anything else that's banned, inform a senior supervisor. And no emotion. If you want to watch the match, go and buy a ticket or go to the pub – you're here to work.'

The fans, when they look at you, are wary; the steward

supervisors are vigilant, staring for any signs of engagement with the game. And the photographers, the television crews, what if you're caught on camera? Nobody wants that. Head down, do as you're told, keep out of trouble. Remember that story – was it ever true? – about the steward who was slashed in the face by a sharpened ring or some other small blade; they say a plaster was put on the cut and he was sent back out to his position. Just keep your wits about you.

'There's Rod Stewart, by the way,' *shouts a Celtic fan, pointing up towards the directors' box.* 'Is the wife with him?' *shouts someone else.* 'Paul Hartley, too.' 'Aye, there's Craig Levein, the Scotland manager.' *It's full already, nearly time for kick-off. The flags are out – tricolours, Union Jacks, Ulster flags, saltires – and then the songs:*

> This land is your land, this land is my land
> From the northern highlands to the western islands
> From the hills of Kerry to the streets of (Free) Derry
> This land was made for you and me
>
> As I was walking by the Shannon water
> Hand in hand with my little daughter
> The church bells ringing, and the children singing
> This land was made for you and me

And from the Rangers fans:

> Though the straits be broad or narrow,
> Follow we will, follow we will, follow we will,
> Though the straits be broad or narrow,
> Follow we will,
> We will follow in the footsteps of our team.

Follow follow, we will follow Rangers,
Everywhere, anywhere we will follow on,
Dundee, Hamilton, even up to Aberdeen,
If they go to Dublin we will follow on
For there's not a team like the Glasgow Rangers
No not one, and there never shall be one
The fucking Celtic know all about their troubles
We will fight till the day is done
For there's not a team like the Glasgow Rangers
No not one, and there never shall be one

The first noise you hear is a distinct metal crack, which carries round the stadium. It is the sound of thousands of metal seats flipping back simultaneously as the supporters stand for their team, and it continues throughout the match, a clear, tinny punctuation to the game's dramas. Minutes before the players emerge, the verse of 'You'll Never Walk Alone' is played over the Tannoy, and the Celtic supporters raise their scarves aloft, pulled taut, as they sing along, grandly, defiantly, in solidarity, and all you can see in the stands is a blanket of lines of green and white. In contrast, the Rangers fans twirl their scarves and boo vociferously, with a stubborn resistance. When the players run out, it is as if the crowd suddenly rages as one; it is unrestrained, brutal, raw, and the only time during the game when all 60,000 supporters share the same sentiment, a release. You feel as though everything around you is lifting, like a rising clamour, and everybody is reaching for something that is beyond them.

The sound then ebbs and flows in response to what is happening on the field or in the stands, but it never ceases. When the Celtic team forms its customary pre-match huddle, the noise intensifies again, to a pitch so vehement it is like a bellow, and the Rangers fans respond when their players run, applauding, towards the narrow corner of the Lisbon Lions Stand that houses all 8,000 of them. The game kicks off and you fall into your practised drill.

Unless the order comes from a senior steward, or the violation is too brazen to ignore, you mostly leave the fans to their own convulsions. It is seldom one lone voice rising to shout Fuck the Queen or Fuck the Pope, and the way to maintain order is to be visible, to be present as an authority figure. Ejecting a fan is messy and tends to rile those around them, so it has to be a blunt breach of what is permitted, in which case it is brought to the attention of a senior supervisor, or grave enough to involve the police – you're not being paid enough to be gung-ho. Provocations are rife, it is the nature of the event, but none of you comes to a football match with a sensitive soul; like most of your colleagues you have an allegiance one way or another, a sly faith that is transmitted in stolen glances with each other, looks that are heavy with meaning depending on the status of the game. You walk up and down the aisles through the game, and remain wary.

The mood in the stands is antagonistic. When Marc-Antoine Fortune's goal is disallowed in the first half, the Rangers fans rise to chant:

> We shall not, we shall not be moved,
> We shall not, we shall not be moved,
> Not By The Hibs, The Hearts or the Celtic,
> We shall not be moved

And as the upper tier of the Lisbon Lions Stand begins to shudder and sway, the Celtic supporters respond with:

Who's the mason, who's the mason,
Who's the mason in the black
Who's the mason in the black

'It's frightening, terrifying, exhilarating and inspirational all at the one time,' says McDade. 'You have to wonder how these guys can stand up out on the pitch let alone play football. The game is seldom enjoyable to watch in the truest sense of the word. It is, equally, the fastest ninety minutes of the week. So wrapped up in the affair are you, so joined to the action like a limpet mine that you daren't check your watch or look up at the scoreboard to see how long there is to go.'

But nobody feels unsafe, there is no longer any sense of peril inside the ground, as there was in the 1970s. The last occurrence of any significant crowd disturbances was in May 1999, when several Celtic fans invaded the pitch at Parkhead, and Hugh Dallas, the referee, was hit by a coin thrown from among the home fans. The game is so stringently policed, and the fans so heavily segregated, that there is little opportunity for violence, and the supporters themselves have little wish to become embroiled in something at the game. They have paid to attend, they want to see the match, and they are representing their club, their own sense of identity.

'The atmosphere is better than at other games, as if everyone realises they have a responsibility to lift the team and to join in,' says Marc Chaplain, a Rangers supporter. 'By now, the nerves have been replaced, or hidden away, and defiance and community volume is the order of the day. One often wonders if the team feels the same level of pressure and expectation shared amongst the supporters. But perhaps this game is a fundamental definition of what it is to be a Rangers fan. For all the focus in recent years on songs which may have naughty add-ons or be slightly south of politically correct, what you often find at this game is a rich variety – a more impressive repertoire – of the whole associated songbook: songs about the Union, monarchy, loyalism and rivalry sitting comfortably with traditional Rangers anthems.'

The chants have an edge, particularly among the away supporters at an Old Firm game, who feel under siege because they are outnumbered. The Celtic songbook contains references to the IRA and Irish Republicanism, and supporters have been known, particularly away from home, to mimic pulling a balaclava over their head, silently cross themselves, then make the actions of a sniper taking aim and firing. The Rangers songbook celebrates loyalism, and references the hunger striker Bobby Sands and the pope. One favourite, 'Hello Hello, We are the Billy Boys' – was banned by Uefa because of the line, 'We're up to our knees in Fenian blood', but the same tune is used to chant 'Edu Edu, Edu Edu Edu', (after Maurice Edu, the American midfielder) instead, as a way to circumvent the ban and so rile the Celtic supporters without being explicitly offensive. The references on both sides are historical and religious in nature, touching upon causes and events that had little or no direct impact on the clubs themselves. But they are considered part of the heritage of Rangers and Celtic, so that singing about battles fought in the seventeenth, eighteenth and nineteenth centuries in Ireland is common in twenty-first century Glasgow.

But there is humour, too. At an Old Firm game in 1994, after Duncan Ferguson, the Rangers striker, had been charged with an assault – he had head-butted Jock McStay, the Raith Rovers full-back, during a match – Celtic fans sang:

> He's tall, he's skinny,
> He's going to Barlinnie,
> Ferguson, Ferguson.

Later that season, after Celtic had lost to Raith Rovers in the League Cup final and Paul McStay, the Parkhead side's accomplished midfielder, had failed to score from the spot, the Rangers fans sang:

> Paul McStay,
> Missed a penal-ty.

'Celtic and Rangers both sing songs about Ireland. I don't have any problem with either set of fans doing this. The authorities need to come down hard on discrimination without trying to stop positive representations of the character of the clubs,' says Paul Brennan, a Celtic fan who runs the Celtic Quick News website. 'I have been discussing the songs debate on the website for years. Most Celtic fans realise the days of singing rebel songs are/should be over, but if the club or authorities want to engage people on this issue they need to do so accurately. Calling Irish songs sectarian when they're not ends the debate. Non-Catholic, non-Irish-heritage people will soon tell you they sing these songs without any sectarian malice. If we want to take the politics out of football, explain the reasons to people and do so evenly.

'My grandfather, who died when I was four, took me to games. Then my dad took me. Religion or going to a Catholic school had nothing to do with it, I had friends and classmates who supported Motherwell, again because their fathers supported the team. Celtic is a huge part of my social life but my relationship with the club varies. Today, it's good for my family. It is an important social activity I do with my brother and 69-year-old father. I sincerely believe that families without football never communicate the way we do. It has been good for me, my brother and dad. I hope it does the same for me and my sons. My closest friends and work colleges are not Celtic fans, I spend more time with Rangers fans. Friendships have been established over many years but we know what subjects are safe and what are not.

'The worst thing is, supporting Celtic has been great for my family, but I'm not sure it will be safe for my sons in the future. I am a practising Catholic but I dispute that Celtic are a club for Catholics and Rangers are a club for Protestants. I believe around forty per cent of Celtic fans are not from Catholic or Irish roots. These fans are as committed to the club, its heritage and mission, as me or anyone. Celtic were established by a Catholic monk but the club is open and always has been. This is why I take exception to misguided comments about the Irish heritage being labelled sectarian. Most non-Catholic Christians I know strongly dispute any association with Rangers and I don't believe Rangers had a religious base. Not signing Catholics for circa eighty years had nothing to do with religion.'

Most supporters grow up with their allegiance to the club, as it is usually passed from father to son, or uncle to nephew, or brother to brother. Occasionally, a child will spurn the team of their parents because their friends support the other side, but mostly the team you begin supporting is a relic of the times when fathers held sway over their households. There are anomalies, too, in the Protestant/Catholic divide, but the supports mostly fall into these categories, because families, religions, communities naturally stick together. It is from parents, siblings and friends that the song lyrics are learned, as well as prejudices, and most anti-Catholic rhetoric stems from a historical sense of having to defend Protestantism against the pope and his spreading religion. Anti-Protestantism does not exist to the same degree, since it was traditionally the majority religion, but elements of the Celtic support express themselves through anti-Orangeism and the derogatory use of the word Hun, which has become their equivalent of the term Fenian, used as an offensive term for Celtic fans.

Although emigration from Ireland enflamed sectarianism in Scotland, the same prejudices are held within individuals with no Irish heritage. Glasgow is a working-class city with a culture of smoking and heavy drinking, and a blatant chippiness that moves from the workplace to the pub to the home. Children follow the example of parents or friends, so that the sense is of a perpetual cycle of antagonism, passing from generation to generation. Even in middle-class circles, among university graduates and professionals, old prejudices are ingrained. They are no longer glaring, but held just beneath the surface, and roused again by the Old Firm rivalry.

'People talk about the offensiveness of the away supports; they're supposed to be,' says Edgar. 'That is what they're attempting to do, they're trying to wind up the opposition fans. They're not so naïve that they think the songs aren't offensive, they're trying to get the home fans angry. There's much more offensive singing goes on at the away end of the Old Firm game. It's designed to provoke a reaction. There's a fairly offensive chant about Jock Stein ['Big Jock Knew', which refers to the allegation that the former Celtic manager was aware of child abuse at the club], because the Rangers fans know it really gets to them. And the Celtic fans' IRA references are distinctly to wind the Rangers support up. The best example was the Famine Song [which includes the line: 'Why don't you go home', in reference to Irish Catholics who fled the potato famine, and was judged to be racist by the Scottish courts], because it was a bit of a nothing song. Apparently it had been about for years, but then it was the Aiden McGeady thing [although born and raised in Scotland, McGeady considers himself Irish because of his close relationship to his grandparents, whose nationality qualifies him to play for the Republic of Ireland], and it was done as a wind-up. Then it exploded and that was it, they'll never stop Rangers fans singing it, and they can threaten all they want, because Celtic revealed the chink in their armour when they said, "This really annoys us." I'm not saying that makes the song right – it is offensive, but the songs are supposed to be offensive, they're trying to engender a reaction.'

Religion is a presence at Old Firm games, but in the way that it provides forms of expression rather than as an influence on behaviour. It is the rivalry that is the motivation, and the offensiveness of the chants (and the attempt to dominate the other side) is a consequence of the game's working-class roots, its sense of itself as hard-bitten, uncompromising. The vast majority of supporters on both sides of the Old Firm divide do not believe they are defending their faith so much as their club; old insults and provocations that linger from previous generations are grasped as part of the identity the fans are embracing. Sectarianism and political resentment is evident in the songs, and the Old Firm rivalry seems to be its last remaining outlet. Glasgow is still a divided city, yet the relationship between football and religion is no longer self-evident.

How can it be, when Old Firm matches are routinely held on a Sunday? In common with much of Britain, Glasgow has moved steadily towards secularism, in the sense that the number of people actively following their religion has been in steady decline. Until the final two decades of last century, supporters would attend their team's match on a Saturday, then the church or the chapel on the Sunday. It has often been observed that football is the new religion, but this a trite over-simplification. There are ritualistic elements to both, a sense that faith and observance will be rewarded, and even a kind of ethical framework in the rules of the game – its disciplinary structure of yellow cards, red cards and suspensions – and the notion that once you have declared your support for a certain team, it cannot be altered; but football does not seek to provide meaning or enlightenment, to explain our place in the world, or to provide moral leadership.

'People search for identities, and there are ready-made ones there, which Rangers and Celtic have utilised in the past,' says Edgar, a former spokesman for the Rangers Supporters' Trust. 'I know people who would describe themselves as Catholic or Protestant, but who wouldn't know what the inside of a chapel or a kirk looks like. There will always be this identity. Celtic have put Irish Catholicism at the head of their agenda. Rangers have tried to ignore anything to do with that, in terms of identity, and the fans have started to push the Scotland thing more. It was unheard of to see a saltire at Ibrox ten, fifteen years ago, and now it's becoming more common. The clubs are searching for an identity, and the fans search for an identity. With Rangers and Celtic comes a ready-made one. Rangers do try to distance themselves from the Protestant, British thing and Celtic have made a move towards the Irish, Catholic thing.'

The relationship between religion and football is complex in Glasgow – a city that still plays host to annual Orange walks. Celtic were formed by and for the Catholic community. Rangers, like the majority of Scottish clubs, were staffed and supported predominantly by Protestants, but religion was not part of the club's ethos when it was founded (there was no involvement from the Church). Instead, when Celtic were formed in 1888 and went on to enjoy a successful spell, Scottish football and society (including newspaper editorials) sought an opposing force to stand up to them in a Protestant v. Catholic encounter that reflected the divide prevalent in Scotland at the time, particularly on the west coast. Rangers were the obvious side to fall behind. The rivalry would have developed anyway, because of the clubs' proximity to each other in the city, but it became inflamed by the religious identity that each came to represent, and the split was entrenched.

'It's tough to say how genuinely religion plays a part in it any more,' says Edgar. 'It's a label these days. I don't think God or Jesus exists at an Old Firm match. Religious labels play a huge part in it, and people's definition of who they are plays a huge part in it. I don't know how many of the 50,000, 60,000 people really believe that what we are watching is a representation [of the struggle] between Protestant hegemony and [oppressed] Catholics any more. But it's there, you hear it. One half's calling the other dirty Orange bastards, the other's calling them dirty Fenian bastards back. There are genuinely bigots on both sides, and I've tended to find the higher the level of bigotry, the less the interest in the football. It would be naïve to say that there's not a religious element to it, it's just a question of how much genuine religion plays a part in it. There's a whole generation now that's grown up secular but uses [religious] terms to describe the opposition fans because that's what they grew up with. A couple of years ago, people found the term Fenian offensive, because it refers to Catholics, but in my experience it wasn't so much Catholics as Celtic supporters. It doesn't make it right, and I'm glad that the word's been eradicated, because it was particularly hateful, and it was supposed to be. But I don't know how many of the younger people used it other than to refer to a Celtic supporter. There are certainly really offensive words on both sides that are starting to [fade away]; you tend to find that the younger generations go Huns and Tims and you tend to find that Fenian is dying out, which is a good thing. You've got to try to drop the religion as much as you can from it.'

The adoption of Rangers and Celtic by football supporters in the north and south of Ireland, almost wholly along religious lines, provides further depth to the rivalry. Again, the two clubs are seen to represent a certain identity, Protestant British and Catholic Irish, in a way that English Premier League clubs are not. Many fans in both parts of Ireland will support a Premiership team and either side of the Old Firm, while Rangers and Celtic supporters' clubs exist in significant numbers across the Irish Sea. And as Celtic have felt more inclined to emphasise their Irish heritage, then Rangers supporters have sought to ridicule it or cleave to an identity that celebrates their British or Scottish heritage.

'Tradition, heritage and roots all have a part to play in football, possibly more so with Celtic and Rangers,' says McDade. 'I genuinely believe that the drama and opera that is the story of both clubs gives people an identity. For my part, I've always viewed Celtic as a Scottish club but with Irish roots. Without labouring the point, I think it's important to stay faithful to roots. Had Celtic been the dream of a French priest from Boulogne who saw the need to form a football club to help with the scourge of poverty in the late nineteenth century, I have no doubt we'd all be standing at Celtic Park eating garlic bread, drinking *vin rouge* and singing the 'Marseillaise' just before kick-off. A Rangers-supporting friend of mine said to me that the Protestant identity had been lost to the Scots due to declining church attendance and less veneration of Ulster Christianity. In his opinion, Rangers, even as just a symbol, are the last bastion of Scottish Protestantism.

'It is the working class who ultimately stick by football, even although club owners often think otherwise. We need heroes with whom we can identify, who go out onto a pitch and make a difference to our day and indeed the quality of our lives. Undoubtedly, the line between the guy on the terrace and the guy out on the pitch has lengthened considerably in the last decade or so. However large the chasm becomes, there is still that feeling that the guy out on the pitch is doing it all for you.'

But there are anomalies. The Dublin Loyal is a Rangers supporters' club based in Ireland's capital, set up by two Scottish fans and an Irishman who supported the Ibrox side. Members include Scots, Irish, Northern Irish, Protestants and Catholics, and although meetings are held in private, there is no sense of them being embattled. There was some consternation, though, when they unveiled a banner during a game against Falkirk at Ibrox in February 2008 that read: 'Dublin Loyal RSC, Behind Enemy Lines'. The phrase was taken from a newspaper article about the supporters' club, and was considered a lighthearted reference to Dublin being considered a city of mostly Celtic supporters, but police officers took the banner down, a stance that was supported by Rangers officials. Both teams have a long history of supporters' clubs, which now reach across to North America, Australia, and almost every other corner of the world that has been reached by the Irish and Scottish emigrants. In Scotland, when one Celtic supporters' club called themselves the John F. Kennedy CSC, it is said that the following week a notice appeared in one of the Glasgow newspapers that carried supporters' clubs information for the Lee Harvey Oswald RSC.

In the 1960s and 1970s, when the two clubs reached five European finals between them, supporters used to travel to the games by any means they could, often taking days to reach their destination in an old, clapped-out bus or car. There are stories of one supporter selling his house to raise the money for the trip, and telling his wife to go and live with her mother. Another is that a group of Celtic fans arranged to stay with the relative of one of the group in France during the journey to Lisbon for the 1967 European Cup final, but they couldn't remember the exact address when they arrived, so walked up and down the street singing Celtic songs until their host came out. After the 1970 European Cup final in Milan, which Celtic lost to Feyenoord, many of the supporters of the two sides swapped scarves, and when they arrived, drunk, at the airport, police put them onto the wrong flights, based on the colours they were wearing. Rangers fans, too, travelled in vast numbers to Barcelona in 1972 for the Cup-Winners' Cup final against Dinamo Moscow, and invaded the pitch afterwards, just as the Celtic supporters had done in Lisbon, although the Spanish police reacted violently. Something similar occurred when the two clubs reached European finals again, with Celtic fans filling Seville in 2003 with good-natured bonhomie, while the city of Manchester was besieged by Rangers supporters in 2008, many of them hopelessly drunk, and some who rioted when one of the big screens showing the game in Piccadilly Gardens broke down.

Since Rangers bought Maurice Johnston, the former Celtic striker, from Nantes in 1989, many of the supporters' favourite players have been Catholics. The religious aspect of the Rangers identity seems based on anti-Catholic rhetoric, and supporters are either ignorant or pointedly dismissive of the songs that they sing in support of their team being offensive to several members of that side, many of whom are idolised. This irrationality is typical of football, a game that is able to powerfully skew the senses of its followers, so that rationality becomes a victim of supporters' passions. Many Rangers fans are more inclined to express their identity through anti-Catholicism – as in songs like 'Derry's Walls' or 'The Sash' – whereas Celtic fans cling to the romantic notion of Irish Republicanism, even if it can no longer be detached from the terrorist atrocities of the IRA, which in turn the Rangers fans find offensive. A sharper political edge entered the songs of both sets of fans during the 1970s, and as the Troubles escalated, but the peace process in Northern Ireland has not stopped songs associated with the IRA or the UVF being heard. Much of the debate that surrounds the Old Firm rivalry becomes stuck in these definitions: what is sectarian, what is political, what is legal, what is morally dubious; and so it becomes an endless swapping of recrim-inations rather than a profound attempt to find a way to eradicate the prejudice.

'Two of the greatest fan heroes of recent years were Roman Cath-olics, one of whom – Lorenzo Amoruso – is amongst the most popular players to have worn the jersey in my lifetime,' says Chaplain. 'I couldn't begin to tell you the religious leanings of most of the players I've watched and nor do I care. I am not religious and nor are any of my Rangers-supporting friends, most of whom are thirty or under and (almost) all of whom are university graduates. I don't think that, even amongst those who still go to the kirk, synagogue, chapel or other place of worship, religion per se plays a real part in their support of Rangers or Celtic – identity is more important. Rangers traditions, exemplified by Mr [Bill] Struth [who managed Rangers for 34 years and was a defining influence on the club], the man and his era, are not about theology, but about how one conducts oneself, about standards, about being proud of hard work and striving to do one's best – these may, in short-hand, be the sort of thing categorised as the "Protestant work-ethic" but this, and the support and affection for Britain, monarchy and Union, is something that remains effective and appealing to many, if not all, in today's support, even although religious affiliation and participation has been reduced.'

The dynamic of the relationship between the two sets of supporters is constantly evolving, even if some elements remain stubbornly ingrained. Celtic fans (and some club officials), for instance, often claim that a bias against them persists among Scottish referees and the game's ruling bodies. This feeling has carried through from times last century when there is every likelihood that isolated individuals would – in keeping with the views of the predominantly Protestant west of Scotland society at the time – be hostile towards the Catholic side. However there is no evidence of an institutionalised prejudice against Celtic in the past – how could there be when the club was so successful? – nor of any discrimination now. There is a sense of the club being aware of this history of Catholic oppression and keeping it within touching distance, even though the chairman in 2010 was a former cabinet member in the previous Labour government, Lord John Reid, and his predecessor was a former governor of the Bank of England, Brian Quinn, two figures once at the centre of the British Establishment. Rangers fans, for their part, continue to mention Fenians, Bobby Sands, and the pope in some of their songs; they denounce Celtic for promoting the club's Irish heritage, but ignore the Northern Ireland flags and scarves carried by their own support. Everything is chosen for its symbolism, and for the offence it will cause the other side.

'Groups such as the Rangers Supporters' Trust have done much in recent years to promote the positive side of the associations between the club and our fans across the Irish Sea, with Ulster-Scots society meetings and fundraisers and parties to highlight and celebrate, amongst other things, the continued success of the Dublin RSC,' says Chaplain. 'Having such a large contingent of supporters coming over from Ulster and more southern areas has always led to the promotion and discussion of ideas and events.'

Contradictions are an inevitable consequence of the reactionary nature of so much of the rivalry; it can never be diminished, as the two clubs so dominate Scottish football, and so the terms of the conflict have to keep changing. What has entered the opposition between the two sets of supporters in recent years is a kind of tit-for-tat points scoring, so that both groups are permanently on the verge of indignation and outrage at some slight or other. Website forums and newspaper and radio phone-ins provide the means to rush to condemnation, and there is, among a minority of fans on either side, a permanent conflict between being offensive and being offended. This extends to the media, with both sets of supporters accusing the written press and other media of bias towards the other side.

'The national broadcaster, the BBC, has consistently adopted an approach towards Rangers the club, and its supporters, which is matched in its hostility only by its consistency,' says Chaplain. 'With a commercial enterprise this is distasteful but easily remedied: should I wish to avoid the [Rupert] Murdoch mantra, I choose not to buy News International products. But when I am forced, by law, to fund an organisation so intent on demonising me and so open in their general distaste for my allegiances, that then is another matter entirely.'

Yet a Celtic supporter would be just as likely to make the same claim against the BBC for pro-Rangers bias. The rivalry so distorts perspective that fans cannot, or choose not to, see the contradiction in singing something to wind up the opposition fans, and then complaining about being wound up themselves. But then so much of the verbal lashing out is defensive, in the sense that the wider vilification of the Old Firm rivalry causes both sets of fans to consider their identity to be under threat. Internet forums have, in many cases, replaced or added to the traditional social conversation about games and teams, and so what once might have been said in private is now publicly on view, creating a further sense of neurosis, even if the online communities are varied and the extremism balanced out by more moderate views.

'I am one of the people who run the Follow Follow website, so one begins to notice attention switch to the game with Celtic a few weeks in advance of the fixture, as people firm up travel plans, complain about the inevitable early kick-off and almost inevitable change of date, and begin to consider the possibility of scoring six or seven in the derby,' says Chaplain. 'In the days leading up to the game the [website] traffic sees a considerable jump – only Champions League games and speculation over signings compare in terms of popularity. Although the various forms of media take a great interest in the Glasgow derby, it is telling that our users seem interested in what they have to say – and how they choose to report – only after the game, where the angle, slant and selection of incidents to high-light can provide for some very heated discussion.

'Perhaps the most remarkable aspect confirmed by the online experience is the worldwide nature of the fan-base: people from every country you can think of – and some you doubt exist – join in the discussion, asking for help in watching the game or simply feeling that this time, above all others, seems right to contribute to the collected memories and thoughts of the wider community.

'It is certainly the case that some of the opinions offered [on fans' websites for both clubs] may be controversial and, owing to the huge number of people registered, often offensive and beyond the mainstream, but is also undoubtedly the case that much sensible, well-organised and well-developed ideas and organisations have found their inspiration in such arenas. The pride felt in setting up the RST, or in collecting tens of thousands of pounds for Erskine [a nursing and medical care home for members of the armed forces], or in developing a network of interested fans to set up the Blue Order or in facilitating a tour to show off the history of the Rangers and its founders: all of these and more are directly attributable to the power of online communities and the passionate fans that use them.'

Walking up and down the aisles, you see how the fans react to each other as much as the game, as though their interactions with each other are as much a part of the Old Firm derby as the encounter between the two teams. The air is cold, clear, but agitated, too, as if thrown into turmoil by the occasion. You can sense the tension. Every goal-scoring chance, every foul, unleashes some of the angst.

A foul that goes against one team is seen as a slight towards the club itself; the referee is treated as though in collusion with the other side. Songs suddenly surge into life, then die out, while individual fans yell at the pitch in a solitary rage. They are mostly oblivious to you, as you walk up and down the aisles, their attention held by the match, or the opposition fans, or some small, personal diversion: 'Look at their bench, who the fuck does he think he is? Sit back down, ya bastard.'

Suddenly there is pandemonium, a huge and abrupt surge of movement and noise. Everybody is off their seats and leaning towards the pitch or hugging somebody nearby. It's a kind of bedlam. Instinctively, you move into position, in anticipation of the crowd's reaction becoming unruly, but also as an act of caution.

On the touchline around the pitch, colleagues stand up to face the crowd, a thin line of yellow rule while they celebrate the opening goal.

You feel like an interloper as the Celtic fans embrace each other, sharing this moment of joy. Then, suddenly, the focus shifts from the players to the Rangers fans, and goading begins, in gestures and songs, as though the goal is secondary to the sense of superiority it provides over the other side.

As the noise and the agitation begins to level out, and you start again to fall back into the routine of surveillance, the supporters become suddenly deflated. The noise now is coming from the away fans, where the bodies are jostling and leaping. Then an angry defiance asserts itself around you. It's resilience from the home fans, a grim stoicism as their frustration mixes with their exhortations to the players, while the away support sings with gleeful pointedness following the equalising goal: 'That's Why We're Champions' and 'We Shall Not Be Moved'.

'You're utterly appalled when Celtic score, because you're in the worst place in the world for it,' says Edgar. 'You're sitting watching them. You look round, there's three sides, you don't want to look at the fans, you certainly don't want to look at the players. But a few seconds, then it's up and into a song. It's the bravado, the shield goes up. Internally, you'll be thinking, "It's against us now, that was a bad one to lose", but outwardly you sing and try to ramp it up as much as you can, and let the team know they're not beaten. If it goes to two or three down, then the singing is all you do, because acceptance kicks in. When you get the opportunity to celebrate a goal, it's carnage. It's like a primal release, because it's just sheer, undiluted joy. It mixes with this feeling of relief, this pent-up emotion, the couple of weeks of build up, it all comes out. It's a group delirium – 8,000 people hugging strangers, you feel part of something. I always feel sorry for people who don't understand football because they'll never get to experience that. It's such a powerful, collective feeling. It's utterly joyous. The reaction to a goal at an away Old Firm match is always the same. It's unbridled joy, everybody punches the air towards the player, who tends to come over to you, there's this great celebration, then as one, everybody turns round and gives the home support the fingers, and it's almost choreographed.'

Liverpool is another west-coast city deeply influenced by immigration from both parts of Ireland. It is working class to its core and in thrall to its two football clubs, neither of which was founded along religious lines, but the rivalry between Everton and Liverpool is less blatantly established. In Glasgow, the religious associations of the two clubs are entrenched, and the division spreads into other areas of life.

'It would be interesting to compare the differences in the [influences of rivalries among other teams] on everyday life, for example, the Celtic fans who refuse to drink McEwans lager [once the sponsors of Rangers], or the Rangers fan who refuses to let his children eat green starburst sweets (yes, really),' says McDade. 'It is not so common to hear of things like that when it comes to other teams and other derbies. It certainly impinges on my life with the family. My wife is a huge fan yet finds it impossible to watch the game as she's devoured by nerves. I've had to phone her sometimes afterwards from Glasgow as she can't even bear to turn the TV on to find out the score.

'The game is always hugely important even if there's nothing at stake. So many things are brought to the party. Bragging rights, oneupmanship, the feeling that whatever the next week throws at you then it's bearable because we've just beaten Rangers. I shout more at the Old Firm game although I'm not a singer. My background is that I became a Celtic supporter as an eight-year-old. At the time I was getting into football, Celtic were the biggest team in the country and I had various uncles who were devotees of the club. I went to a Catholic school where, famously, I remember there being only one Rangers supporter, although the janitor was reckoned to be a red, white and blue aficionado. Again, in those days, Celtic were the biggest team in the country, Rangers were in a slump and I suppose there's a natural glamour for young boys to back winning teams. It still goes on. I know there were a lot of young boys turned on to Rangers for the same reasons in the nineties and that includes kids who went to Catholic schools. The sway of Gascoigne, Laudrup, nine titles in a row, holding appeal for them.'

Supporters of both halves of the Old Firm are politicised in ways that must seem bemusing to other football fans. Because the two clubs now represent two distinct parts of Scottish society – Protestant/ Unionist and Catholic/Republican – they cannot be considered solely as sporting institutions. When a group of hardcore Celtic supporters called The Green Brigade displayed a banner at Parkhead denouncing the poppy symbol being displayed on the players' jerseys during Remembrance weekend in 2010 (in keeping with the gesture of many other British football clubs, including Rangers), Scotland's political and social commentators were hauled into an impassioned debate about free speech, about what it means to be British, about what the poppy stands for – all prompted by a banner at a football match.

Rangers and Celtic are institutions, standing for something more than comradeship and shared emotion. What is expressed during an Old Firm game is the instinctive need to stand for something, to be worth something, which is then shaped by the historical distinctions between the two clubs. That these identities are religious in origin, and so susceptible to prejudice and fear, makes them not only more intense, but also more far-reaching. Where other football rivalries can be deeply felt, no others are so rooted in society itself, where the same division once lay more strongly, and so is still detectable.

'Why it matters is a slightly complicated issue,' says Chaplain. 'There are a large number of different types of Bluenose. Many view Rangers as part of – perhaps as the sporting manifestation of – a wider set of beliefs and bodies, encompassing loyal orders, the Church of Scotland and others. An increasing number of younger Bears [Rangers supporters] are simply interested in the football – although not dismissive of the influence of the past, they find no cause to affiliate themselves with other, traditional complementary philosophies. The route of father passing [his allegiance] on to son is familiar, but interestingly among my peers not as common as might be anticipated. Regardless, the intensity of feeling seems to be extreme amongst many of those who support the Rangers. Not a day goes by without me talking, thinking, writing or worrying about my club. In some senses that is clearly ridiculous. A true football fan has to be critical. Human beings certainly are hard-wired to believe certain things to be true or to find some arguments and attachments to be more beneficial than others – so perhaps it is no surprise that the emotional bond with the football club is often seen to be more powerful than those of more traditional relationships and communities.'

You look at your watch: five minutes remaining. As if automated, stewards pour onto the trackside round the pitch, and stand shoulder to shoulder around the perimeter, looking into the stands, watching. You see their faces, impassive, and know what they are thinking: almost over now, we're nearly there. When the final whistle sounds, you move to the top of the aisle to let the supporters wash out of the ground quickly, and an eerie silence comes to fall

quite suddenly on the stadium, a sudden respite. You still feel
enclosed when you begin to fan along the seats, clearing the rows
and looking for anything that has been left behind. The worst job
is clearing the toilets, which tend to be sodden and full of empty,
if not smashed, glass bottles of vodka, whisky or Buckfast.

You then join your colleagues in gathering around a senior
supervisor at the bottom of the main stand for a debrief, and still
you say nothing about the game or the result. 'Did anything
happen today?' the supervisor asks curtly. 'Did anybody see
anything that they had to act upon? Well, thanks for your efforts,
you did well today.' But the mood remains solemn, even among
the stewards who follow one team or the other. You catch someone's
eye and there is a brief, knowing look, but that is all.

'The horrible truth is that football fills a void in Glasgow and the
west of Scotland. You can be poor, violent, socially inept, you can
lose family, friends and social standing, but you never lose your right
and ability to support a football team,' says Paul Brennan. 'People in
this category cause problems in every city in the world but here they
also support football. This is not football's fault, and Glasgow is not
alone in having this issue, but football has to cope with it. After the
game my mood is totally dependent on the result. I'm never nasty
after a defeat but it's hard to be happy. I don't like to talk about a
defeat and tend to answer questions about the game with a closed
comment, not inviting further conversation. The streets are not safe
the night before or after a Celtic–Rangers game. I know several Celtic
fans who have been attacked when isolated. Drink has a major part
to play but the issue is wider than that.'

It's as if the game continues to run, in the debates about contentious decisions, about mistakes that were made, about who played

well and who did not perform, as though supporters feel a need to keep it alive. As the fans head away, it is to their homes or to pubs that they know will be full of their own kind, because the match is still influencing their behaviour.

'I know it's a really sad thing to say, but if you're going drinking, the result dictates where you go,' Edgar says. 'If it's been a tense match as well, that makes a difference. If you've rolled them over 4–0, you can go wherever you like, because the Celtic fans will retreat back to the Celtic pubs, and if Rangers have been beaten, the Rangers fans will go to Rangers-friendly pubs. If it's been a controversial match, I tend to avoid the city centre, because you know there will be a higher propensity for bother, because there will be anger as well as alcohol. The result is quite important, and the circumstances of the match, in determining what you do. But how it can make you feel the day after is bizarre, there's no other football match like it. When you've won, you get up the next day and you're buzzing, you can't wait to get into work, there's a regal air about you, a big smile on your face; whereas if you've lost, you're angry, you're annoyed and you know you're not going to get a chance for revenge for another two or three months. It's a very unpleasant feeling and it doesn't shift, even for the next couple of results. I've seen us play a match against Celtic, lose, and even after a couple of decent victories we're still talking about that game, the things the manager didn't do right, the things the referee didn't do right. It sticks in there.'

CHAPTER 4
THE DUGOUT

Walter Smith is sitting in the main stand, his arms wrapped tightly round his torso as he watches the game begin to unfold. The Rangers manager's face is pensive, his eyes wary, while he chews slowly and discreetly on a piece of gum. His seat is at the end of a row at the front of the Celtic Park directors' box, and to his right is Ian Durrant, the Rangers first-team coach, who is wearing the same thick, grey club jacket, and whose expression also flickers between attentiveness and unease. Smith prefers to watch matches from the stand because he can see more of the game from a wider perspective than down at the touchline, but nervously shifts his position from time to time, as if always on edge.

By the side of the pitch, Tony Mowbray is standing with his hands in his trouser pockets, leaning against the edge of the Celtic dugout, with one leg crossed in front of the other. He is wearing a smart dark suit and jumper that isn't able to conceal the physical bulk of the centre-half he once was. His eyes are narrowed and his chin juts out with a kind of defiance. Eventually he is overcome and the play drags him out to the touchline to shout an instruction to his team. When he moves, he seems bent over slightly, and he looks less imposing.

The two managers are confronting each other, but at the same time they are separated: by age, experience, achievements, their sense of job security, even the habit of Smith watching from the

stand and Mowbray from the dugout. What they carry with them
into this game is a personal history: Smith, the elder statesman
at sixty-one, with twenty years as a manager, a slew of trophies
and a reputation so established and gilded that it would survive
the loss of an Old Firm game, or even a league title. He has
worked with Jim McLean, Graeme Souness and Sir Alex Ferguson,
and even those Rangers fans who grumble about his cautious
tactics recognise his accomplishments and his place in the club's
history – as the manager who led the team to nine league titles
in a row, and the 2008 Uefa Cup final. Mowbray is forty-six and
has only been a manager for six years, although he won the
Championship with West Bromwich Albion in 2008. But he has
yet to fully establish his worth at Celtic, despite the promise
shown during his spells in charge of Hibernian then WBA. The
pressure is on both men, but it seems more of a burden to
Mowbray, a manager still seeking to prove himself in this most
demanding of environments.

Smith is in his second spell at Rangers, already having led the
team to a league title, two Scottish Cups, the League Cup, as well
as the Uefa Cup final since returning in 2007. The club, then, was
in turmoil as the short reign of Paul Le Guen ended in broken
relationships with senior players, and with a team that was already
adrift in the Championship race. Smith was brought back to revive
a club that was in a state of despair. In his previous spell, he won
seven titles (as part of the record-equalling nine-in-a-row), three
Scottish Cups and three League Cups. His career is defined by his
success at Ibrox, and he has brought a measured authority to the
business of managing the club at a time when the club's large debt
to Lloyds Bank effectively saw the entire team being made available
for transfer.

In his shrewdness, with his cold, hard stare and his dry wit, Smith
is a man typical of the west of Scotland: unprepossessing, reserved,

Fans make their way to Celtic Park on a cold Sunday morning in January 2010 for the first Ne'erday Game in 10 years. © SNS Group

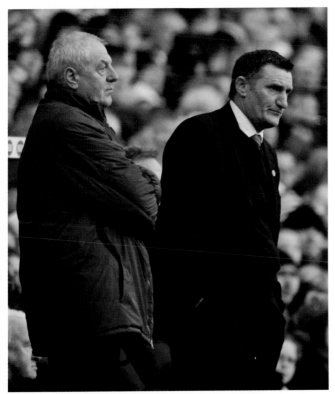

Walter Smith, the Rangers manager, and Tony Mowbray, his Celtic counterpart, watch pensively from the touchline at Celtic Park. © Getty Images

The Rangers and Celtic supporters are separated by stewards and police at Celtic Park. © SNS Group

Photographers train their sights on the action as part of the vast media coverage of the Old Firm game. © SNS Group

Medical staff and helpers attend to injured fans at the Ibrox Disaster, when 66 Rangers supporters died in a crush on Stairway 13. © Mirrorpix

Frantic efforts are made to treat people hauled from the crush on Stairway 13. © Mirrorpix

Stairway 13 at Ibrox after the crush that saw 66 Rangers fans die at the end of an Old Firm game. The metal barriers were bent by the sheer weight of people trying to leave the ground at the same time. © Trinity Mirror/Mirrorpix/Alamy

Mo Johnston, the former Celtic striker, sits next to Graeme Souness on the day he is unveiled as a Rangers signing, breaking a long-held if unofficial tradition of the club not signing Catholics. © SNS Group

Paul Gascoigne mimics playing a flute, which is symbolic of Orange Walks. After this, the English international received a death threat. © Getty Images

Members of The Dublin Loyal, a Rangers supporters club based in Ireland's capital, display their flag with the statement: 'Behind Enemy Lines', which they were asked to take down by stewards. © Willie Vass

Chris Woods, the Rangers goalkeeper, clashes with Frank McAvennie, the Celtic striker, at an Old Firm game in 1986. Terry Butcher is also involved. All three ended up being sent off during the game and, with Graham Roberts, later appeared in court. © SNS Group

A Celtic fan dresses as the Pope, reflecting the club's Irish Catholic heritage, but also the constant urge of Old Firm supporters to wind each other up. © SNS Group

Rangers fans show their humour at an Old Firm game by poking fun at the failure of Neil Lennon's side to win a trophy. © SNS Group

The Celtic huddle, which the players perform before every kick-off and which prompts a roar of support from their fans.© SNS Group

Ally McCoist, the Rangers assistant manager, and Neil Lennon, the Celtic manager, confront each other at the end of an Old Firm Scottish Cup replay in March 2011. © Willie Vass

Neil Lennon reacts to the taunting of the Rangers supporters by cupping his ears, a typically defiant gesture. © SNS Group

A Celtic fan shows his support for Artur Boruc, the Polish international who became known as the Holy Goalie after blessing himself in front of the Rangers fans. © Matthew Ashton/AMA/Corbis

Celtic and Rangers fans clash on the pitch at Hampden following the 1980 Scottish Cup final, a riot that led to a ban on alcohol sales at football grounds in Scotland. © Donald MacLeod/Scotsman

capable of great warmth but also an instinctive aggression. His Rangers team is a reflection of these qualities, and is consequently awkward to overcome, while his Old Firm record at this stage is bettered only by Jock Stein and Scott Symon (two managers he later overtakes), and Willie Maley and Bill Struth. At Celtic Park, it is enough for Smith's side to avoid defeat, having won the season's previous Old Firm game 2–1 at Ibrox and built up a lead at the top of the Premier League. Smith is an assured presence, protected by his reputation but also the solid, uncompromising displays of his team. He is more detached than he was in his first spell as Rangers manager, delegating much of the training to Ally McCoist, his assistant, and Kenny McDowall, the first-team coach, while often toying with the media, confident in his use of on- and off-the-record briefings to reveal details about the club's current precarious financial state and the influence of Lloyds Bank.

Smith's experience and stern air of command have become sources of faith for the Ibrox support. There is, too, a pragmatism to his style of leadership, an element of resourcefulness that combines with his man-management to draw the best out of players. Working at Dundee United under Jim McLean, he used the training ground and relied on his coaching ability to drill players, to enable them to carry out the manager's tactical schemes. Smith carried out the same role as assistant to Graeme Souness at Ibrox, before succeeding to the main job himself and then using the club's generous resources to bring richly talented players to Ibrox like Paul Gascoigne, Brian Laudrup, Andy Goram and Stuart McCall, and letting them play by cajoling and inspiring them, while setting standards of commitment and determination that had to be maintained. His second spell at Ibrox has called upon his skills both as a coach and a motivator as he integrates hard-headed older professionals like David Weir, Sasa Papac and Lee McCulloch with younger, more erratic talents such as Kyle Lafferty, Maurice Edu,

Steven Whittaker and Steven Naismith; only Steven Davis, Allan McGregor, Kenny Miller and Madjid Bougherra can be said to be in the prime of their careers.

Smith is both a patriarchal figure – as revealed by the number of his former players who remain captivated by him and call him, still, 'Gaffer' – and an autocrat. A glance can be cold and unnerving, while he is capable of sudden bursts of anger. In the dressing room over the years he has raged in players' faces, kicked a steel kit hamper across the floor and hauled players against the wall, but these were calculated acts of fury designed to fire up his players, to focus them, or even to emphasise the obligation on both halves of the Old Firm, which is to win every game, whatever the circumstances. Smith's greatest achievement was never allowing his players, or himself, to become jaded by success. Having grown up as a Rangers supporter, often travelling from his home in Carmyle to Ibrox with his grandfather, the history of the club and its fans is part of the background of his life. And it is this grasp of the need to keep winning, to keep churning out results, that has enabled Smith to be so successful. It is reflected, too, in his Old Firm record, with his teams outplayed at times, particularly by Tommy Burns' Celtic side, only to find a way to win the game with a Laudrup goal or a Goram penalty save. This bloody-mindedness, or refusal to concede, is the char- acteristic of a Smith side: his teams are tough, uncompromising and unforgiving.

'If you win, everybody likes you, if you lose they don't, you just have to realise that's the situation and handle it,' Smith has said about the demands that come with being in charge of Rangers. 'The manager is there to protect the players and make sure they don't get badly affected by the levels of criticism. A lot of the boys who come in are surprised at being put under the microscope. They can play in Scotland for a number of years, then they join the Old Firm and find that their performances are dissected, analysed and criticised, and that affects them. They've never had that before. It is different. The [Old Firm] clubs are linked, whether they like it or not. You always have a respect for everybody that takes on the positions as manager. It's a difficult job. There are five million people in Scotland and football is one of the biggest things newspaper-wise. It's quite a claustrophobic environment to work in, and a difficult environment to work in. I don't find it a great problem. You get people coming up, but they're normally very nice. They ask for an autograph, or want to talk about that day's game. If there are aspects of the job you don't like, don't do it. It's not just the media, they mirror the pressure coming from the supporters. You have got to be prepared to take a fair amount of criticism.'

Tony Mowbray is where Smith once was: coming to terms with the intensity that surrounds the Old Firm, and the pressurised environment that he has to manage in. He is the rookie, and an embattled one, to Smith's veteran. Mowbray succeeded Gordon Strachan the previous summer, returning to the club that he once served as a stoic centre-back, and bringing with him a commitment to a certain style of football. Mowbray is an idealist, however much he attempts to distance himself from this label. His approach is shaped by the conviction that the style of football a team plays is vital, so that he considers it essential for his team to pass the ball from the back, to perform with poise and attacking intent, even a degree of haughtiness. He should have been a perfect fit at Celtic, where a certain romanticism is contained within the stories of the club's formation, its association with a Catholic community that struggled to find acceptance, in the Lisbon Lions of 1967 – the players Jock Stein drew from within a thirty-mile radius of Celtic Park, and who became the first British side to win the European Cup – and in the reverence towards gifted players like Jimmy

McGrory, Jimmy Johnstone, Kenny Dalglish and Henrik Larsson.

Mowbray brought with him an emotional connection with the supporters, having met and married a Glaswegian girl called Bernadette Doyle who died of cancer while he was still playing at Celtic. The fans came to revere him, as he would often only leave his wife's hospital bedside to play for the team (despite losing 17lb in weight), and for the dignity and resolve he showed in the wake of her death. It was Mowbray, too, who introduced the huddle before games kick off, when all eleven players gather together in a closed circle and bond during a final message of inspiration from the captain. For Mowbray, it was a gesture of solidarity at a time when Celtic were struggling off the field due to financial problems and in-fighting among directors, while Rangers were moving inexorably towards nine in a row. The supporters respond to this act of unity, raising a cheer that is both defiant and hostile (to the opposition) as the players briefly hunch together. Even Rangers players react to it at Celtic Park by waiting until it is over, then jogging towards their own fans, applauding, and so holding up the start of the game in a kind of retaliation. Yet for all the symbolism and sentimentality of Mowbray's background, and his reputation as a rugged and fierce defender, in management he has become grave, sober and ideological.

At Hibernian he worked with a group of emerging young players full of talent and brazenness – among them Steven Whittaker, Kevin Thomson, Scott Brown and Derek Riordan, who would all play for the Old Firm – and instilled his principles of deft, attacking football. At Easter Road the expectation is to aim for the upper reaches of the table, and so the philosophy could be implemented under less pressure. Mowbray took his beliefs to West Bromwich Albion, where his side became characterised as one that played slick, engaging football, but that was also fragile in spirit and defensive integrity. After a game against

Everton at Goodison, Mowbray received a letter from Bill
Kenwright, the Everton chairman, describing West Brom's
performance as the best he had seen at the ground. Yet still they
lost. It was this sense of a flawed idealism that Mowbray brought
to Celtic, and of the lessons not having been learned. There was
also the widespread belief that the club, however much they
denied it, wanted Owen Coyle then Roberto Martinez to succeed
Gordon Strachan, but the two managers chose to remain in
England. Mowbray, too, was obliged by the board to retain Neil
Lennon on the coaching staff, and the impression that quickly
emerged was of a manager who was compliant, who could be
dictated to by the Celtic directors. In the opening five months
of his reign, his side had created chance after chance in games,
but failed to take them, while looking vulnerable at the back. In
comparison to the hard-headed doggedness of Rangers, a team
capable of grinding out a result whatever the circumstances, the
image of Mowbray as a dreamer, somebody too entranced by his
own vision, was further embellished.

A spiky relationship with the media, which he so often looked
startled by despite having lived in Glasgow for four years as a player,
contributed to the uncertainty around him. Mowbray already
appeared to be a manager lost to adversity, and his touchline expression – often mournful, or bleak – became emblematic. At times,
he even seemed bemused by the demanding nature of the role, and
his own position as a figurehead, as though it felt overwhelming.
In comparison with the steadfast and composed Smith, he appeared
ambivalent, forlorn even. In Glasgow, this air of vulnerability has
developed into a predicament for Mowbray. The goodwill and
esteem that built up during his playing career at Celtic Park carries
no influence now, not when results and the club's ability to compete
with Rangers are at stake. He is exposed here, in a city where he
should be at ease and thriving, and it is leaving him pained, as if

he is despairing. His only consolation is commitment to a set of coaching principles, however besieged they might be.

'We need to win week-in, week-out, but we will try to do it with a style that makes the supporters proud to follow this football club,' he said when he was unveiled as manager. 'I'm here to be successful and win things for Celtic. Some managers will tell you that they are there to win football games. But I want to achieve both – I want to win as well as entertain. I want Celtic supporters who come along to the game to leave matches happy at the way their team performed and the way their team tried to play. I want the fans all over the world watching games on TV to feel the same. There is no magic wand. You can't change from one style of play to another overnight. It takes plenty of hard work on the training ground. The size of the support, the tradition, the history, are all the things I hold true when I talk about footballing philosophies. Since the club started, Celtic have generally tried to give their supporters entertainment, score goals, win trophies and play with a style and a panache about them. And it just felt right for me. I will try and put my stamp on the team and try and give the supporters something back. I watch Iniesta, Xavi, Messi and great players like that. That is what inspires me. I need to be inspired as well and the supporters need inspiring. When I watch Spain, Barcelona, great technical teams and players, I try and recreate that where possible. I can't make a Lionel Messi out of a player. But the best football teams are a unit, a group of individual players who understand their role within the team. That is only achieved on the training ground and that's what we hope to work towards.'

All these people behind me, looking at me, counting on me, savaging me; and all these players in front of me, carried away by the commotion of the game. The referee, making decisions based on what? His impulsiveness? The pressure of the crowd? Who's in charge of this game? Who's in charge of these teams? Who's in charge of these players? Not me, nobody can bloody hear me. How long have we played? That much already? Christ, where does this game go?

That's a goal, referee, that's a goal. For fuck's sake, are we ever going to catch a break from these guys? Do they know the game? Have they ever even played it? We needed that, it was our breakthrough, we have them on the rack. They can't cope with us. Ohhhh Jesus, that tackle, that's a bad one. He's hurt, that's a terrible foul. Referee. Referee. There's no place for that. Take control, for Christ's sake. We need to get on the ball more, move it to the flanks, get them in behind. If that doesn't happen, I'll need to change it. Ten minutes into the second half, I'll prepare them at half time. No, maybe fifteen or twenty minutes in, I don't want to leave us vulnerable. But then what if that's not long enough to make the change worthwhile? Aw referee, for fuck's sake referee, that's a foul. Where's the fourth official? 'Hey, what about that challenge? That's a clear foul. A clear foul.' Come on, I can't believe you didn't see that.

It was only hours before the Old Firm were due to kick-off in the League Cup final, on 26 October 1986. Darkness had already fallen outside Hampden Park on this midweek evening when Davie Hay approached David Syme in the stadium's foyer. 'I want to congratulate you on the way you handled the 4–4 draw [with Rangers] last season,' the Celtic manager said.

'Thanks,' the referee replied warily.

'Now, that Ted McMinn dives all over the place,' Hay added. 'I hope you keep your eyes on him.'

Hay's Celtic team were about to come up against Graeme Souness's Rangers, a side containing newly signed England internationals Chris Woods and Terry Butcher, and only four months into the manager's transformation of Ibrox and the horizons of Scottish football. Like any Old Firm cup final it was a significant occasion, but this one also seemed freighted with meaning: Hay's side would have to stand firm against the momentum of Souness, whose arrival was a disorientating experience for the Scottish game. He brought ambition and implacability, which was both suited to the Celtic v. Rangers rivalry, but also dangerous. The Ibrox side had not won the league for eight years, and Souness was appointed to drag the club into a new era; his bullishness, conceit and fury were a direct challenge to Celtic, the defending champions. Souness also had money to spend, and his capture of Butcher – who had been a target for Manchester United – and Woods was seen as a bold statement of his ambition. Yet Hay was able to send out a side full of attacking guile and prowess, with players like Brian McClair, Paul McStay, Mo Johnston and Mark McGhee. This final, coming so early in the season, was an opportunity for Celtic to respond to their headstrong and striving neighbours.

Souness represented glamour and a preening self-assurance: the midfielder who played with such fierce aplomb for Liverpool's European Cup-winning sides, then went to Italy and fitted seamlessly into a culture of refinement and elegance. Hay was more rugged, more typically Scottish; a popular and feared midfielder, part of the Quality Street group of Celtic youth players, along with Danny McGrain, George Connelly, Kenny Dalglish and Lou Macari who came through to replace the Lisbon Lions. An aggressive competitor, Hay earned the nickname, the Quiet Assassin, for his brutal treatment of opponents. As Celtic manager, he won the 1985 Scottish Cup and the league title the following season, but the arrival of Souness was a renewed and more searching challenge. The outcome of the final, even lifting the trophy itself, seemed secondary to the consequences of victory and defeat on the two sides as they continued on to contest the league title. Hay was a calm, if uncompromising and occasionally forceful figure on the touchline; tall, and robust, but seldom overcome by rage. Yet at Hampden his self-restraint could not contain his growing fury with Syme.

Once the game kicked-off, Rangers took the lead through Ian Durrant, a young, skelf-thin midfielder with a carefree and precious talent, only for McClair, already a gracefully devastating and shrewd forward, to equalise eight minutes later. The game was tense and the increasing suspense of the second half, along with the beseeching passion of the 74,219-strong crowd (the capacity at the time was 74,000), caused the encounter to spill over into a confusion of anger and resentment. Both teams were so desperate to win that the game took on a frantic quality.

Then, with eight minutes left, the referee awarded a penalty when Butcher fell in the penalty area while being challenged by Roy Aitken. Davie Cooper converted the spot kick, and as they sought to find another equaliser, Celtic became anxious. When a free kick was awarded, Johnston confronted Stuart Munro and appeared to thrust his head towards the Rangers full-back, a gesture seen by the linesman. Syme had already booked a number of players including Johnston, and he showed both players the yellow card, which meant a red for the Celtic striker. The decision infuriated Hay, who stormed towards the touchline while the Celtic striker – his shorts pulled up tight and his socks rolled down to his ankles – blessed himself as he walked off. Then Syme felt a blow on his back, turned round to see Tony Shepherd, the Celtic midfielder, and sent him off, believing he had punched him. Startled, Shepherd pointed to a fifty pence piece that had been thrown from the stands and tried to explain that it was the coin that had hit the referee, who realised his error and allowed Shepherd to remain on the field.

As disorder reigned, Hay walked onto the pitch and picked up the ball.

'Things can trigger you off,' Hay later said. 'Any Old Firm game can have that effect on a manager but there is a trophy at the end of this one. Sometimes there can be an instance or an incident in a game which can send you off. Normally, you try to be calm and collected but it can make you react a little differently. I remember that final in 1986 and, to this day, I think I was proved right and the referee made a mistake in giving Rangers a penalty. It was a really tight game and one or two controversial decisions proved decisive. Most people must have thought I'd lost the plot, but I was trying to be a calming influence. But when I saw the referee, you might put it mildly and say I reacted a bit differently from what I thought I was going to do. That hinged on the fact the decisions were the difference on the day. I was more wound-up about that match than any other during my time as manager. I don't think I can ever forgive [the referee] for what happened in 1986. It was bedlam, utter chaos. At one stage I was left with the ball in my hands after Mo was sent off. I have to confess that for a split second I thought about volleying it at the referee. That's what an Old Firm clash can do to you. It's easy to become irrational if you believe that forces are against you. On that particular day the match official totally lost the plot. It was a shame because up until he decided to take centre stage it hadn't been a bad game. I couldn't believe what was happening when he sent off Shepherd. I heard Syme saying: "I've made a mistake." I felt like saying: "You're one big mistake." The refereeing in that game was diabolical. I was involved in head-to-heads with John Greig, Jock Wallace and Graeme Souness during my time in charge, but I always had respect for them and I'm sure they had respect for me. We always shook hands at the end of the game no matter what had happened during it. I was always more likely to fall out with the ref rather than the opposing manager because, to be honest, the bosses don't really have any control of what's happening once the first ball is kicked.'

After the cup final, a still incensed Hay said to the media that Celtic should move to England, a comment that resonated with the sense among the club's fans that they were discriminated against by officials. Years later, Syme admitted in a private conversation that he might have made a mistake awarding the penalty, and Hay has never lost the conviction that Scottish referees are under too much pressure and scrutiny to handle Old Firm occasions. He even backed the idea of foreign referees being appointed to Rangers v. Celtic games, because they wouldn't face accusations of bias.

The pressures of managing the Old Firm can distort the temperament and judgement of even the most self-possessed individuals, and the job can seem all-consuming, with an endless tumult of drama, gossip, criticism and hysteria around the football clubs. While Celtic manager, Hay grew concerned about the regular presence of Johnston on the front pages of the newspapers – the striker was a renowned nightclubber with a ready charm and burgeoning celebrity that tended to attract plenty of female company – and persistent rumours of drug-taking, so he tested the player's urine. Johnston was unaware of the ploy, believing instead that it was part of an extensive but routine medical check-up, and the tests came back negative. Yet the suspicion, the pervasive innuendo that swirled across the city, the subterfuge and the sense of gravity, were all direct consequences of the agitation around the Old Firm, the constant white noise. 'When you've played for Celtic you realise how big a club it is, how much it means to people,' Hay has said. 'It's their lives. It's only when you're involved that you realise how big a job it is. You've got a responsibility for the massive support that follows Celtic.'

There is little to be said in the dressing room afterwards, some words of praise or encouragement, maybe even a rebuke or two, but the analysis of the game can wait until the next day at training. We have come through it. The press are upstairs, but they can keep waiting. They'll be after the usual stories: winners, losers, heroes, villains. Plenty of refereeing controversies – he can take the flak today, that's what they can have. The chief exec will be sidling around somewhere, but he can wait, too; there's nothing to be said. The manager's office, that's where to go. The last time I was at their place and they won, three or four former players all turned up, smiling, joking. Aye, very funny, I know what they were up to: gloating. Still, we'll have a laugh, it's good, all of us together, sharing the moment. Nobody knows what it's like, even the coaches; they can at least go home and blame it on me. There's only two of us who can properly understand. And how many times have I heard it said: I can't take many more of these, I'll call it a day at the end of the season. But then we never do. It always seems retrievable then, or the success is overpowering. It's ego, isn't it, the belief that you can thrive in this job, in this city, in this rivalry? Ego and fear, that's what it is.

When Liam Brady became Celtic manager in 1991, he began to grasp the magnitude of the role when his appointment was an item on the main evening news, not even kept back for the sports bulletin. His wife, Sarah, glanced across at him with a look of concern: 'Are you sure you know what you're doing here?' But then nobody can be really certain about how the job of managing Rangers or Celtic will affect them; it is a test of character, of strength of will, of diplomacy, of psychology, of man-management, of how to be the figurehead for an entire community of people, many of them with long-established views about how the role should be carried out. Davie White, John Greig, Brady, Lou Macari, Dr Jo Venglos, John Barnes, Paul Le Guen – all found their spells in charge cut short. The obligation is always there to win trophies and matches, particularly Old Firm games, and to be a figure of authority and leadership, but every reign is different. There are boardroom pressures, financial constraints, difficult players, vocal fans, even awkward coaching staff to deal with; it is a political position, with social responsibilities as well as the day-to-day demands of the game. An Old Firm manager can be asked about domestic violence in the aftermath of derby matches, or sectarian singing. Even triumphant Old Firm managers eventually have to face disdain from their own support, as the drive for success is relentless. How can it be any different when the two clubs measure their worth in trophies, with one, Rangers claiming fifty-four league titles, and the other, Celtic, forty-two?

'I didn't buy well, and you live and die by your purchases as well as your results in the eyes of the fans,' Brady later reflected. 'I genuinely believed I had the knowledge, so it was a rude awakening. I was too inexperienced to handle it, but Celtic turned out to be a manager's graveyard for several who followed me. Glasgow is a demanding, aggressive city, and although I didn't achieve what I'd hoped to, I've no regrets about that particular period of my career. To have managed a winning team in an Old Firm derby is something no one ever forgets. When you come from where I come from [in Ireland], you know all about [the religious nature of the divide]. The responsibility was huge; you're not only a footballer manager of Celtic, you're a leader. That community is depending on you to win trophies to make their life all the happier. Of course, when that's not happening, the pressure is enormous. At Celtic, you have to win.'

History is an opponent, too, in the sense that the influence of several managers from the past can still be felt at both clubs. Willie Maley spent forty-three years as manager of Celtic, amassing a haul of thirty trophies by the time he left in 1940 and setting standards at the club that are maintained to this day, particularly the notion that the Celtic way is to play attacking football, to be fearless. It was Maley who built the foundations of the club with his dictatorial style, demanding and accepting only the very best from his players, but he was matched, at Ibrox, by Bill Struth. Their reigns overlapped, with Struth taking charge of Rangers from 1920 to 1954, and he also won a total of thirty trophies, so that the two men stand as the most successful of all managers in Scottish football. Like Maley, Struth was a product of his time: stern, authoritarian, a stickler for convention – he demanded that his players adhere to a strict dress code that included a bowler hat – but he also ensured that Rangers became known for their sense of superiority. He insisted that the players behaved and performed as though they were the best in the country, and also that they were treated that way by the club (in all but money, since footballers were little more than regular employees at the time).

Yet for all that Maley and Struth were the pre-eminent figures in the early years of both clubs, one manager still dominates the recent history of Celtic and Rangers, as well as Scottish football as a whole. Jock Stein was a modestly talented but committed centre-back whose playing career amounted to little but who achieved greatness when he moved into management. Stein steered Celtic to the very forefront of the European game, and at the same time began a tradition of gruff but successful Scottish managers that includes Sir Alex Ferguson and David Moyes. Stein was of the same generation of Scottish football men as Sir Matt Busby and Bill Shankly, men who emerged from a mining background in Lanark-shire to revolutionise their football clubs; Stein was their equal in many ways, and their better in having beaten them to the European Cup.

So much nostalgia has attached itself to Stein because of the nature of the team's victory over Internazionale in 1967, when the Scottish side – all pasty faces and skinny bodies – prevailed over the athletic, bronzed Italian team in the heat of Lisbon through their attacking intent and refusal to be cowed. But Stein was a colossus of a manager, and for all his conviction that the game should be played to entertain, he was prepared to compromise in the pursuit of success. Stein's Celtic also won nine league titles in a row (as well as one further league title, eight Scottish Cups and six League Cups). That is the haul of a manager who is hardened and ruthless; Stein could be a fearsome figure, and he often intimidated his players and the press when he felt the need to exert his authority, but he was also prepared to be indulgent, once confiding in an unguarded moment that perhaps his greatest achievement was prolonging the career of the extravagantly gifted but wayward winger, Jinky Johnstone. Stein was forever rescuing the player from scrapes and dramas – he had a network of informants who let the Celtic manager know which pubs Johnstone was drinking in so that he could rebuke the player by phoning the bar and asking the landlord to hand Johnstone the phone – and Jinky repaid him with the exuberance and wilful brilliance of his talent.

By the end of the 1990s, both Old Firm clubs were reliant on foreign players, and when Dick Advocaat took over from Walter Smith at Ibrox in 1998, he brought a different sensibility to the job of Rangers manager. The Dutchman was forthright, curt and at times dismissive. He was enthralled by the sense of grandeur at Ibrox, the way he was greeted by the doorman on a visit – 'Good afternoon, Mr Advocaat' – the oak panels and the marble staircase inside, the tradition of wearing a suit and the club tie. The order and the convention appealed to a manager who was stern and disciplined, but also to a man who was sentimental. Yet Advocaat took time to come to terms with the Old Firm rivalry and the harsh nature of its divide. During his early months at Ibrox, he made several expensive and high-profile signings as he rebuilt the Rangers team, but kept returning to a particular target, the former Celtic striker Pierre van Hooijdonk. Both Advocaat and Arthur Numan, the Dutch full-back who was the manager's lieutenant in the dressing room and an international teammate of Van Hooijdonk, tried to persuade the forward to return to Scotland, only to keep being told that it was impossible. Advocaat even accused him of being scared.

'In time, you'll understand the situation between the Old Firm,' Van Hooijdonk told him. 'One day you will realise I am right.'

Advocaat met the striker soon after his side clinched the league title in May 1999 with a 3–0 win away to Celtic, a game in which Hugh Dallas, the referee, was hit by a coin and fury gripped the home fans. Advocaat shook his countryman's hand and said: 'Now I understand what you meant.'

The Rangers team bus took such a circuitous route back to Ibrox that Sunday afternoon – because the security officials and police were so concerned about Celtic fans attacking it – that the journey took three hours, when normally it would be little more than thirty minutes. Advocaat was the first foreigner to manage Rangers, and although he'd experienced the great rivalries of Dutch football, between Ajax, PSV Eindhoven and Feyenoord, the intensity and extent of Glasgow's divide was a revelation. His first competitive match was against the Irish side Shelbourne in the Uefa Cup, and the game had to be played at Tranmere Rovers' Prenton Park ground, near Liverpool, rather than in Dublin, for security reasons.

Advocaat was eventually worn down by the job, after Martin O'Neill's arrival at Celtic ended the Dutchman's run of two consec-utive titles and restored the Parkhead side to prominence (O'Neill won their first encounter 6–2 at Celtic Park, Advocaat the next 5–1 at Ibrox), but the passion of the city and its supporters, even the edginess of the rivalry, became something of value to Advocaat. 'You cannot compare that with Holland,' he later said. 'The love the people have for Rangers and Celtic is so deep and so real that you feel it as a manager. I did not know it, but I realised that when you are the manager of Rangers or Celtic, you are something special. Religion is for every individual, so I stayed away from that. Once, when I was at the Hilton hotel for dinner with my wife, I went to my car and three Celtic [supporters] took their trousers down, in front of my wife [to moon at the couple]. I just said, "Thank you".'

Only twenty-nine men have been Old Firm managers, and they have all come to feel exposed by the job. Willie Maley was succeeded by Jimmy McStay then Jimmy McGrory, neither of whom could live up to the standards their long-serving predecessor had set (they won one league title between them in twenty-five years). Stein restored a sense of triumphalism to the club, as well as the identity of the team being bound up in its ambition and style, and he was followed by Billy McNeill, the captain who had led Celtic to European Cup glory in Lisbon and who then guided them to three league titles as manager. Part of the fabric of the club, and steeped in its history, McNeill remains a figurehead for Celtic supporters, even the current generation who know him only through the re-telling of his exploits.

Struth was followed by Scot Symon, another authoritarian figure – players were only ever admitted into his office at Ibrox to be censured for some misdemeanour or other – but also a manager who maintained the club's sense of entitlement. During thirteen years in charge, he won six league titles, five Scottish Cups, four League Cups and twice took Rangers to European Cup-Winners' Cup finals, losing on both occasions. It was Symon who set up the famous trophy room at Ibrox, and who brought the gifted, if rakish, Jim Baxter to the club, as well as John Greig, one of Rangers' greatest servants. But Symon also suffered a Scottish Cup defeat to part-time Berwick Rangers in January 1967 that remains the worst result in the Ibrox side's history, and was sacked nine months later. His successor, Davie White, lasted only two years and is one of only two Rangers managers (along with Le Guen) not to win a trophy with the club.

While Stein was leading Celtic to nine-in-a-row, Rangers were struggling to regain their poise, and it took the return of Willie Waddell, a right winger who played under Struth and, briefly, Symon, to restore some purpose to the Ibrox side. He spent only two and a half years in charge, but in that time took Rangers to their greatest triumph: the 1972 European Cup-Winners' Cup final win over Dinamo Moscow. Waddell immediately stepped down to allow his assistant, Jock Wallace, to take over, another famously strict and demanding manager, but one whose players responded to his gruff man-management. Wallace, a former soldier, led Rangers to two trebles in the space of three seasons, and ended Celtic's run of dominance, only to resign unexpectedly in 1978 after a dispute with the board.

John Greig stepped up to become Rangers manager in place of Wallace. He once met his wife off the train from Edinburgh to go shopping, and after they'd walked down the street for a few yards, a man shouted, 'How you doin', big man?' Five minutes later, another shouted: 'You Orange bastard.' There is no respite.

'It's all-consuming, it's exhausting, it's so demanding,' said Billy McNeill, who managed Celtic in two different spells. 'The pressure is just incredible, and if things don't go well it is absolute hell. But if you are successful it is the most satisfying job in the world. The fans demand success – they are an emotional crowd. But if you achieve anything you are a hero for life. You couldn't go for a game of golf during the week, because there would always be somebody wanting to talk to you and tell you what they think. There is no way to hide. You just have to accept that people know who you are, they know where you are, and they want to help you at times.'

McNeill understood intuitively what was demanded of a Celtic manager and his team, having grown up in the west of Scotland as a supporter of the club, then spending his entire playing career at Parkhead. The late Tommy Burns also served Celtic as player and manager. He, too, appreciated the social and cultural influences of the club, and the manager's role as a figurehead. He once remarked that as an Old Firm player, half the population of Glasgow believes that they own you, while the other half hates you. He also described his career as playing and managing 'for a people and a cause'. Yet Graeme Souness had little real understanding of what he was taking on when he agreed to become manager at Ibrox in 1986. Souness grew up in Edinburgh, and his only knowledge was that Rangers were a big club that needed reviving. He accepted the offer of a player-manager role before leaving for the 1986 World Cup finals in Mexico, then agreed to the board's suggestion that Walter Smith, the Dundee United and Scotland coach, would be an excellent assistant manager.

The reality of the job, its demands and its antagonisms, was perfect for Souness, an arrogant, pugnacious and self-assured character. But the confrontations and constant skirmishing with the football authorities and the press eventually became a drain on his energy and his health. Souness lasted five years in Glasgow before, exhausted and stressed, he accepted the offer of a return to Anfield to manage Liverpool. Yet he was a critical influence on the Ibrox side, hauling them into football's new era of money and celebrity with the sheer force of his ego and charisma, while being determined to demolish the last of the club's old traditions by signing a high-profile Catholic player. His capture of Mo Johnston in 1989 not only relieved the Ibrox side of its Protestant-only straitjacket, but also crushed the Parkhead side's spirit.

'I didn't know what I was getting into, I didn't know the politics. I just knew that it was a big football club,' Souness later said. 'It's the hardest job in British football, because if you're top of the league and not playing very good football, the pressure's off. You can be second, have a couple of bad refereeing decisions, one bad day at the office when you get beaten by someone and you end up being second, but you're playing the better football. The pressure all goes on the second team, and it's how the players, management and the directors all handle that spotlight and pressure of being second. That can bring you down. I hadn't experienced that before. I quickly realised the pull Rangers has on its supporters. It goes way beyond football. It's an institution. You're born a Rangers supporter, you die a Rangers supporter, you only watch Rangers, you only buy Rangers paraphernalia. Divided city, divided country in many ways.'

Foreign managers have brought a different sensibility to the job, a perspective that is not shaped by the enduring tensions of the rivalry. But they are often made starkly aware of why some conventions have become established. Dr Jo Venglos went to watch a Rangers game after becoming Celtic manager and sat in amongst the fans, who quickly made their antagonism clear. It was not customary for Old Firm managers to watch the other team from the stands. And Le Guen was spat upon by a Celtic fan when he went to watch the Parkhead side play Hearts at Tynecastle.

John Barnes had been a successful player for Liverpool, Newcastle and England when he was approached by his old friend and mentor, Kenny Dalglish, to become Celtic head coach in the summer of 1999. It was to be Barnes' first managerial position, and he accepted that there would be some resistance to a rookie coach taking the job at a club of Celtic's size and stature. But the presence of the director of football, Dalglish, a Celtic hero, was supposed to be a source of comfort. Instead, Barnes faced constant enquiries about Dalglish's involvement, with the expectation that the former

Liverpool manager would be more hands-on, and Barnes quickly sensed that he was in an impossible situation. He held on until February 2000, when a Scottish Cup defeat at home to Inverness Caledonian Thistle saw him sacked. 'As much as you think you know [about the pressures], you don't until you're involved,' he said about the Celtic job. 'It's passionate. I'd been to a Celtic v. Rangers game, so I knew the fervour, but until you're in it you don't really know it. I was a first-time manager and a lot of people thought I shouldn't be there. Even after the first eleven games, when we'd won nine, lost one and drawn one, we were four points behind Rangers and it still wasn't very positive. So I thought, "If this is what it's like when we're doing okay, what's it going to be like when we're not doing well?" At certain clubs, they like an affiliation. I understand how much the club means to the fans. In Glasgow, they either love you or hate you and the animosity was much worse in Glasgow than Liverpool. It's not personal, it's just the nature of life in Glasgow.'

After Barnes, and a temporary spell in charge for Dalglish, came Martin O'Neill, a Northern Irish Catholic with a growing reputation for astute and inspirational management from his achievements at Leicester City. The job was ideal for O'Neill because he was ready for the challenge of managing a big club and because Celtic were in a state of disarray compared to Advocaat's Rangers side. O'Neill was also fiercely intelligent and perceptive; he knew what the religious divide meant, having grown up during the Troubles, but also what Celtic represented to the Catholic community, since his dad had been a supporter. In his character and his strength of personality, O'Neill was a natural leader, and he became a messianic figure to the Celtic fans. He transformed the fortunes of the team so abruptly that they defeated Rangers 6–2 in only his fifth league game in charge, but by then O'Neill had been exposed to the competitive tension between the two sides. Rangers had played their opening game of the season on a Saturday, and won, then Celtic travelled to Dundee United the following day, where O'Neill took part in a pre-match broadcast interview at Tannadice. 'If you lose today,' he was asked, 'would the season be over?'

Instead, his Celtic side containing Henrik Larsson, Chris Sutton, Joos Valgaeren, Stilian Petrov and Paul Lambert secured a 2–1 victory, then was further strengthened by the signings of Neil Lennon and John Hartson. O'Neill went on to win the treble in his debut season (becoming the first Celtic manager to achieve the feat since Jock Stein) and then the double the following year. In 2003, he led Celtic to the Uefa Cup final in Seville, which they lost 3–2 to Jose Mourinho's Porto, but which saw thousands of Celtic fans take over the city and celebrate their team.

O'Neill was always conscious of the history he was becoming a part of, the depth of feeling that the club inspires, and one of his first acts as manager was to take the Lisbon Lions team out for dinner. This immediately endeared him to some of the most influential voices around the club but also acquainted him with all the current tensions and personalities in the dressing room and beyond. O'Neill was a shrewd manager, but also an insightful one, something Dermot Desmond later articulated when he said that the Northern Irishman immediately took 'mental ownership' of the club.

'I remember when I had signed the forms and the crowd was waiting outside [Celtic Park],' O'Neill later recalled. 'It had started to rain and I thought, wouldn't it be fantastic if we could win something, because the supporters were ready for it. They had taken the time to come out of their homes and offer their support. That excitement went right through me and that evening felt like the start of something. I've watched a lot of derby games, but Celtic v. Rangers is something else. You worry yourself to death about it at least four days in advance. You try to keep a cool head and it's really important to have a bit of discipline around the game. I remember Walter Smith once saying that he felt that his first feeling was one of relief if they had won, and then maybe once in the dressing room there's a bit of euphoria. That's an apt description. You don't want to lose the game and that feeling when the final whistle has gone is mixed, one of relief and one of elation. It's a great footballing city, in Europe, if not the world.'

Alex McLeish replaced Advocaat at Ibrox in 2001, with the Dutchman taking on a short-lived role as director of football. He played a significant role in identifying McLeish, who was then in charge of Hibernian, as his replacement, but also made sure that his successor knew what the job entailed. 'They came for me,' he said to McLeish about the press. 'And one day they will come for you.' Yet McLeish understood the demands of the job, having grown up in Barrhead, a town outside Glasgow, as a Rangers fan. He enjoyed immediate success, arriving in the December and winning the League Cup and the Scottish Cup, defeating Celtic in both competitions along the way. The following season, McLeish won the treble and he added another title and League Cup in 2005. But as Rangers were downsizing due to the lavish spending that David Murray, the chairman and owner, had embarked upon during Advocaat's reign, McLeish then had to reduce his squad and seek out bargain signings. The circumstances were harsh, and by the time his former Aberdeen teammate Gordon Strachan was appointed Celtic manager in July 2005, McLeish was coming under increasing pressure. The two men were close friends, as were their wives, having spent six years together at Pittodrie under Alex Ferguson, but the Old Firm rivalry meant their relationship had to change. They could not socialise together, and ended up communicating by the occasional text message, often when one had suffered a setback, such as Strachan's Celtic being defeated 5–0 by Artmedia Bratislava in his first game in charge. 'Chin up wee man,' McLeish sent in a message to his friend, but by the following year McLeish had been replaced by Le Guen, while Strachan was racking up three league titles in a row, the first manager to enjoy that run of success since Stein.

Strachan spent four years at Celtic, and they were often strained. He was edgy with the media, and many Celtic fans were reluctant to embrace him because he made it plain that he was not a Celtic man (he grew up supporting Hibs) and there was a lingering resentment of the way he and his Aberdeen teammates contemptuously overcame the Old Firm in the early 1980s. Yet Strachan also endured a difficult relationship with Glasgow itself. He often clashed with members of the public who he felt were disrespectful, such as the Rangers-supporting father and son who verbally abused him at a petrol station, and the man he had thrown out of Celtic Park during a tour of the stadium for making a snide remark. There was a fieriness to Strachan that was central to his success in management, but also led to confrontation, as did his sarcastic line in humour. In the end, it felt as though Strachan and Celtic (and Glasgow) had tolerated each other enough when he left in 2009, to be replaced by Mowbray.

'The paranoia, you don't get that in any other country,' Strachan said after he departed. 'The whole west of Scotland thing if you're not brought up in it is mind-blowing. You're either one or the other, and that goes through all walks of life. Where I used to park my car in the mornings, I'd sometimes get a ticket if I was late and sometimes not. It depended if [the traffic warden] was a Celtic or a Rangers supporter. When Walter [Smith] came back [to Rangers in 2007] I asked him if it was different. He said it was completely, it was horrific – the media thing, the internet, rumours on chat rooms, which we never had before. He said it's changed completely. You have to understand that fans get nervous, because they see their club losing things. They react in different ways, sometimes strange, or violent or negative. There's an intensity in every high-profile job. The paranoia sets in with the Celtic supporters, Rangers supporters are paranoid about that referee, this referee. The ugly head is there all the time. There's only maybe a few who are neutral, and that goes through all walks of life. I'd never come across that in my life. There's an intensity, but a nastiness with it. And some people make it difficult for the [majority]. I couldn't handle [children being cheeky]. I chased kids from one side of the cinema to the other in Leeds, to confront them, [because] bad manners is the one thing that annoys me in life. That's me as a person. I wouldn't change it for the world. I came across five or six incidents that were unpleasant in a social setting, but you balance that against the number of people I had laughs with, the Glasgow humour. The enthusiasm of the people, they're funny, but they get aggressive at times.'

CHAPTER 5

THE CONTROL ROOM

At eight o'clock on the morning of Sunday, 3 January 2010, Chief Inspector Wayne Mawson arrives at London Road police station. Ten minutes later, he is standing in the conference room and beginning a briefing to his command team. He runs through the logistics and the tactics of the day's operation, and a checklist of expectations: the routes supporters will take to and from the stadium, the likely numbers of both sets of fans, the significance of the match, and what he demands of his officers. 'Our primary concern is public safety,' he says. 'Our focus is on getting fans to the ground safely, letting them enjoy the game and getting them home afterwards. The fans police themselves pretty well. They know where they can go, they know the safe way home – it's passed down the generations – and ninety-nine per cent of the fans want to come to the game and enjoy watching it. They don't want any bother and they want us to take executive action at any sign of trouble.'

Wayne Mawson is a self-possessed man, circumspect, with a clear, precise manner. His hair is neatly cut, his gaze is bright and unwavering, and his expression is one of firm certainty, as though nothing could cause alarm. He is brisk in his manner, and on the day of an Old Firm game, every movement and interaction in the station is snappy and terse; the atmosphere feels animated, as though to hesitate for a moment would somehow be disruptive. The match commander takes direct control of an area that runs up Fielden Street, as far as Bridgeton Cross, and 250 yards north of Celtic Park towards the M74, taking in the stadium and the roads that immediately surround it, including rows of terraced housing and industrial units.

The operation – The Plan – is meticulous in its preparation and detail, the culmination of two months of consultation, and worked out down to the smallest consideration, even which street corner an individual constable will stand at before, during and after the game, and what his demeanour should be when he interacts with supporters. It is a category-C fixture – the highest risk – and Mawson is in charge of 282 officers from his own command, B Division, and a further 278 drawn from every other force in Strathclyde. This includes support services, riders from the mounted division, traffic police and officers manning the barriers that are erected after the final whistle to corral opposing fans in different directions on their way home. But, always, strategies are drawn up for the worst-case scenario.

It is 10.13 a.m. and word has been passed to Mawson about a march that is about to take place. It is the first unanticipated event of the day. A group of Rangers supporters are walking up London Road from Bridgeton Cross to Celtic Park, approaching the stadium along a route normally used by home fans. Do they have flags? Banners? Is there an intent to cause trouble? The information is vague. Mawson decides to send his football intelligence officers out, and in full uniform so that they are conspicuous and domineering, but also because most of the supporters will know their faces anyway. The officers gather up a side street next to London Road police station, all wearing luminous yellow jackets, all looking wary and sombre, and wait for the Rangers fans to march.

'We have to be prepared for any eventuality,' Mawson says. 'We've always got to keep officers as a contingency in case anything happens.' Experience has made him phlegmatic. For twenty years he was an officer with the Metropolitan Police, the last four of which included being match commander at White Hart Lane, the home of Tottenham Hotspur, before moving to Glasgow in 2008. North London derbies between Tottenham and Arsenal are similar in their demands, even if the rivalry lacks something of the raucous intensity of the Old Firm, that bone-deep sense of antagonism. Mawson is wary of unknowns, the variables that disrupt The Plan. In the weeks leading up to the fixture, he has worked to limit these unanticipated elements. There has been regular contact with Ronnie Hawthorne, Celtic's safety officer, and Kenny Scott, who holds a similar role at Ibrox; with Strathclyde Passenger Transport, to ensure that buses and trains will be running as normal; and with Glasgow City Council, to request that all the roads and pavements around Celtic Park have been gritted in case of snow. Pubs in the vicinity of Celtic Park, and elsewhere across the city that are known meeting places for Old Firm fans before and after the game, have been visited by constables and the landlords instructed not to let drinking or boisterousness become uncontrollable. Police officers have also called upon regular domestic violence offenders throughout Strathclyde, as abusive incidents are known to rise on the day of Old Firm games. The aggressors are identified and, in their own homes, warned: 'Don't even think about it. If you cross the line, you will be arrested.'

The march by a group of Rangers fans is an unexpected complication, but the essence of Mawson's role as match commander is to be wary of complacency, as if a dire occurrence is always just on the verge of happening. As it turns out, only a small group of supporters meet up to walk along London Road to the stadium, and they are easily marshaled by the officers Mawson set aside. But two other issues were already troubling him before the day of the game arrived: the weather and the date. Scotland is in the midst of a cold snap, with temperatures often reaching as low as minus 16 overnight and heavy snowfalls closing roads and schools. Most lower division football matches across the country have been cancelled for several weekends due to the severity of the conditions. It is, by every measure, a freakishly intense freeze. Contingencies can be made for the ice and snow on the ground, but the date itself is a more sensitive consideration. The Ne'er Day fixture was once part of the routine of the Old Firm, but they had become difficult matches to contain because supporters, unrestrained by not needing to work the following day and by the lingering self-indulgence of the Christmas period, were more inclined to discard their inhibitions. They drank more, they allowed themselves to be more inflamed by the occasion, they grew angrier and more aggressive. This was the first Ne'er Day game in ten years, with a Bank Holiday Monday the following day. 'If you see anything that you think could evolve, do something,' Mawson instructs each one of his officers forcefully. 'You have my executive authority to take action there and then. Tell me about it, for officer safety and the safety of the crowd, but do something. Don't ever do nothing.'

At 11 a.m., Mawson makes his way to Celtic Park and embarks on a walk all the way round the outside of the stadium. He visits each of the pre-match deployments, where some of his senior officers are in place and already engaging with supporters. There are 560 officers under his command, working inside and outside the ground. Mawson talks to each police representative that he meets, whatever their rank, looking them in the eye and gauging their mood. If anybody seems uncertain or on edge, he becomes concerned and spends more time with them, running over their duties, their contingency plans, and where their positions should be during the course of the day. At almost 11.35 a.m., he heads inside the stadium.

The Celtic Park control room is in the main stand, jutting out at the corner with the East Stand, and overlooking the narrow swathe of Rangers supporters hemmed in on either side by two lines of segregation, each ten empty seats wide. The crowd is never still, it teems with expressions of emotion. On occasion, the outbursts look choreographed, with every individual understanding how to act, what words to sing, where to address them. More than two-thirds of the ground – the home fans – sing:

> Low lie the Fields of Athenry
> Where once we watched the small free birds fly
> Our love was on the wing
> We had dreams and songs to sing
> It's so lonely 'round the Fields of Athenry

Then the other third sings its own riposte:

> King Billy's on the wall
> King Billy's on the wall

He stands so high, he shines so bright
He lights up the Falls
There's millions come to see him, they stand and gaze in awe
They remember 1690, King Billy's on the wall.

Everything is managed as much as it can be. In the weeks leading up to the game, supporters' groups from both sides seek Ronnie Hawthorne's approval for their banners. They know, generally, what will be considered acceptable – no sectarian slogans or images, no vilification, no swear words, nothing criminally offensive – but if something is close to the bone, then Celtic's safety officer adjudicates. He cannot see them all before the game, so some are viewed in the hours before kick-off and he makes an immediate decision on their suitability. Among those in the crowd are: 'boyd – goal machine. stick your henrik larsson up your arse' in the Rangers end, and 'jungle bhoys support artur boruc – blessing yourself is not a crime' in the Celtic end. Several Scottish, Irish, Northern Irish and English supporters' clubs are also represented by banners or flags.

Mawson stands in the corner of the control room, impassive in that officious way, and watches the CCTV monitors to his right capturing grainy, jagged movements. His gaze is fixed on the screens, watching with a practised eye for a small pocket of people acting independently of the rest, being more aggressive, more hostile, or reaching for something: a bottle? A coin? It's a sixth sense, this awareness, something intuitive that reads an expression or an action and feels that it will lead to something malicious. He sees something. 'Start recording that,' he instructs brusquely. 'And send a steward in. Officers be ready to assist if required.' The focus is on the crowd, but everybody in this tight, enclosed space is aware of the game. What happens on the field impacts directly on the fans, and so in turn on how the police react and manage the occasion.

It is 12.30 p.m. precisely. The game kicks off. The atmosphere in the control room is tense. It is built on two levels, behind large glass windows that look out over the pitch. Downstairs, the Celtic staff sit to the left, manning their own CCTV system and the PA to the stewards, while the police officers – an inspector, a sergeant, and three constables – and their equipment are on the other side of the room, which itself looks out onto the main stand and the East Stand. From this eyrie-like structure, positioned high above the throng of the fans, Mawson can narrow his vision right down to individual seat rows. Next to nothing passes unseen, and everything can be recorded.

The upper floor is split into two. Behind a glass partition, paramedic and St John's Ambulance staff man their own, smaller control room, directing the teams around the stadium to anybody needing medical assistance. A senior officer from Strathclyde Fire and Rescue is also in attendance, along with police engineers, who maintain the radio network and hardware. All remain linked into The Plan, seeing what the others are seeing, listening to what the others are listening to, and following the routine of the occasion.

When the home side wins a corner, supporters stamp their feet in unison while slowly, rhythmically chanting: 'Cel-tic. Cel-tic. Cel-tic.' It feels as though the entire stadium is shuddering. Mawson narrows his eyes. He is looking for trigger incidents, events that can provoke a response within the crowd that has to be acted upon. They can be a movement, a gesture, a small act of disorder, caught on camera or by the naked eye of somebody in the stands and reported back. He makes a mental note of the area of the stadium containing the most agitated fans, immediately works out where his closest senior officers are and which of them would be the most suitable to deal with the situation. If needs be, an evidence-gathering team, equipped with video cameras, can also be deployed. And how would the crowd react to a sudden surge of police presence? What is the balance? How is it best maintained? Mawson stands, remaining still, watching, while these considerations occupy his mind. Waiting for the next trigger incident.

On 2 January 1971, there is a heavy chill in the air around Ibrox, and a deep, forbidding winter's gloom. Even though the Old Firm only meet twice a season in the league at this time, the game between Rangers and Celtic, in front of a crowd of 85,000, is uneventful, the kind of derby encounter that seems unable to rise above the mundane. Minutes before the end, a Bobby Lennox shot bounces off the crossbar, and Jimmy Johnstone, the iconic Celtic winger, heads the ball into the net. Around Ibrox, dismayed Rangers supporters begin to surge towards the exits.

Stairway 13 is at the north-east side of the ground, a notoriously steep incline leading towards ground level outside that had been the scene of several serious accidents during the previous ten years, one of which caused two fatalities. It quickly fills with supporters, all of them intent on leaving the game and the defeat behind as quickly as possible. Then Colin Stein, the Rangers striker, equalises with a powerful shot from inside the penalty area. It is, effectively, the last kick of the ball, and the roar of the home fans can be heard outside the stadium, a mixture of relief and jubilation, something primal.

A reporter stands in the press gantry of the Ibrox main stand, phoning his match report through to a copy taker. A newspaper strike means that fewer journalists are present than normal, and already most of them have clambered down the spiral staircase that leads back inside the main stand to the press room. As he speaks to the copy taker, dictating 800 words in a slow, steady stream, the reporter notices that a growing crowd of people has gathered at the top of Stairway 13. For more than ten minutes, the group does not move. 'What's the problem?' he asks the constable standing at the police control point at one end of the press gantry when he has finished his phone call. It had been a subdued match, with only two arrests made during the game, for drunkenness, and eleven outside, but the police, under the command of Joe Beattie, the detective superintendent who led the investigation into the Bible John murders, are suddenly involved in a catastrophic incident. 'There has been an accident on Stairway 13,' the officer replies anxiously. 'Many casualties.'

Ibrox Stadium at the time is a sweep of terracing, the slopes of the stands stepped and containing barriers for supporters to lean against. When Stein equalises, the reaction of the crowd is so passionate that many of the fans who are leaving turn and try to walk back up to the terracing. But then the final whistle blows almost immediately, and everybody on the terraces starts to make their way out. Stairway 13 is a narrow route leading down to the exits, and as supporters approach it from three different directions, the volume of people is immense. It is always a tight squeeze on the way out of the ground; supporters brace themselves for being pressed together, and fathers tell their sons to raise their arms, so that they cannot be trapped. But on this occasion something is different. Nobody is certain what prompts the crush that is more intense than normal – did two joyous young fans just toss their scarves into the air, then crouch down to the ground to scramble around looking for them, causing other supporters to fall over, or was that a boy who fell from an adult's shoulders? – but the pressing weight of this mass of people is quickly becoming intolerable. Already, it is squeezing the life out of its victims, some of whom are dying while still standing up. One supporter, at the top of the stand, sees an elderly fan stumble and roll down the embankment next to the stairway, helpless.

Supporters begin to shout, 'Get back, get back.' But the momentum of the crowd – many of whom are not in control of their movement, with their arms and legs pinned to their sides – is inexorably in one direction only, down towards the exit. Voices fade as the sound of twisting, grinding metal escapes from the crush; it is a horrifying, screeching noise, piercingly ominous. The barriers of the stairway break, and the great mass of people falls forward, as though drawn into a hole. Soon, there is no screaming. Scarves and coats, hauled off by the crush, fall to the side of the stairway. A terrible silence falls upon the struggle. Bodies – many of them children – are being propelled along the squeezing mass of people, as if carried on a tide. There are occasionally frantic movements, people try to free themselves from the weight of thousands of bodies all herded into a confined space. Most are being moved against their will, their feet lifted off the ground. One man stands on something soft and looks down to see the body of a child; another escapes because he is wearing slip-on shoes and so is able to wriggle free, in a panic, from the crush of people.

Within only a few minutes, corpses have begun to pile up at the bottom of the stairway, twisted together, many of them wearing just socks as their shoes have been sloughed off. When a police officer pulls a young boy from beneath several bodies, the constable begins to cry uncontrollably.

A sullen fog descends on the stadium as the emergency services begin to deal with the tragedy and come to terms with the extent of the toll it has taken. Dead bodies are laid down across the pitch, unidentified, in a bleak line of distress, covered by sheets, or jackets, or towels. By now, news of the accident has reached club officials, and members of staff return to the pitch to try to help. They are not prepared for the sight that greets them. Among the helpers are the two managers, Willie Waddell of Rangers and Jock Stein of Celtic, and they immediately join the medical staff in tending to the wounded and moving bodies on makeshift stretchers down to the pitch. Once some kind of order has been imposed, the two men carefully climb up the terracing to look down on the scene of the accident for themselves. Because of the falling temperatures, a cloud of steam rises from the still warm corpses. There is a haunting silence, as if the sight is so horrifying that it cannot be understood. 'It was like Belsen's piles of concentration camp victims,' Waddell later recalls quietly, haltingly. Some of the deceased have been trampled on and will only later be identified by their dental records, or their tattoos.

Having already left the stadium, most of the players are unaware of the tragedy. A message is relayed to the Rangers dressing room for the team to hurry up with their bath and clear the area. John Greig, the captain, and Sandy Jardine, the defender, are among the few still changing back into their clothes when bodies begin to be brought in to the impromptu morgue. Alex Miller, the Rangers midfielder, was not selected for the game, but had arranged tickets for ten friends. Three of them died, including the manager of his former boy's club, who had stayed at Miller's house the previous night. The medical staff of both clubs work alongside the emergency services – all of Glasgow's hospitals are placed on disaster alert – to tend to the injured in the Ibrox dressing rooms, gym and laundry. Tears stain the face of Celtic physio Bob Rooney as he attempts to revive one victim.

Soon enough Glasgow begins to hear of the accident at Ibrox. The Old Firm divide is breached by the tragedy, its indiscriminate nature causing grief across the city and beyond. Anxious parents, wives and girlfriends wait in their homes for supporters to return, many of whom have headed straight to the pub and so are among those not to have heard the news as it filters out on the radio. On a train from Glasgow to Edinburgh that evening, there is a sombre, listless atmosphere in each of the carriages. Nobody is aware of the true extent of the disaster, only that something terrifying has happened, something that will break the heart of the city. Two men sit together on the train; one, a Rangers fan, weeps while resting his head on the shoulder of the other, a Celtic supporter.

In the weeks following the accident, Old Firm players and officials, often together, attend memorial and funeral services – 65 in four days (one was private at the request of the family) – and many Rangers staff visit grieving relatives. The toll is 66 people dead and 145 injured. One woman, 18-year-old Margaret Ferguson from Stirlingshire, is among those killed, along with 5 young boys from Markinch in Fife who met up before the game, as always, with other school friends who were Celtic fans to walk to where both sets of rival supporters' buses leave for Glasgow. The oldest victim of the tragedy is 49, the youngest a 9-year-old boy from Liverpool.

Supporters' associations from both clubs raise funds for the victims and their families, and a tribute match is played at Hampden between an Old Firm Select – including Bobby Charlton and George Best of Manchester United as guests – and Scotland. The overriding sense is of sorrow for people who had merely set out to watch a football match. There are isolated incidents of anger, though, with one injured Celtic supporter reported to have shouted at hospital staff who he believed were deliberately ignoring him: 'Protestant [bastards].' A requiem mass is held in Glasgow by Archbishop James Scanlan that prompts Pastor Jack Glass, of the Church of the Twentieth Century Reformation Movement, to describe it as an insult to the memory of the Protestant dead.

In 1977, a vast refurbishment programme is begun at Ibrox, led by Waddell and based upon Borussia Dortmund's Westfalenstadion. It takes four years to complete, costs £10m, and results in a 45,000 all-seated capacity. The stadium is awarded five-star status by Uefa. A bronze memorial now stands outside the ground, in the vicinity of where Stairway 13 once led, carrying the names of all the victims. The disaster remains vivid in the memories of all those connected with that day, as something they cannot fully comprehend.

'I don't like talking about it much,' says Colin Stein, the scorer of Rangers' equaliser. 'For a while I carried around the burden that my goal had caused it. The inquiry found that not to be the case. But what a terrible, terrible day. . . Margaret Ferguson, she was the only girl among the sixty-six who died. She'd been in my house just a couple of weeks before. Our daughter Nicola had just been born and Margaret – who we didn't know, she was just a fan – chapped the door with a teddy bear for her.'

It is 1.10 p.m., and only five minutes remain before the half-time whistle will be blown. Officers begin to assemble in the tunnel area, waiting for the call to walk out onto the trackside and fan round the perimeter of the pitch. Mawson remains motionless, with Ronnie Hawthorne and his deputy, David Barron, standing next to him on the left. A Rangers official appears in the cramped space, to make sure that the match is proceeding smoothly enough. All eyes remain focused on the screens. There is little conversation beyond the passing of requests or instructions. In one ear, Mawson receives a constant stream of comments and updates from officers inside and outside the ground, then he sends his officers and the stewards out onto the trackside, in readiness for half time.

The policing of Old Firm fixtures is now a slick operation, following The Plan and The Log, both of which are updated and modified after every game. But Mawson and his officers do not ever lose sight of the potential for disorder. There is always the fear that something catastrophic can arise from a small prompt through sheer momentum, although the majority of the incendiary provocations occur on either side of the segregation lines inside the stadium, where the two sets of supporters are in confrontation.

Much of the rivalry is good-natured, or at least lacking a savage edge, compared to the 1970s, 1980s and into the 1990s, when violence invariably followed an Old Firm game, either inside or outside the stadium, and glass bottles would fly from the terraces, often onto the heads of fellow supporters but on occasion towards the players on the pitch itself. In recent years, it has been more common for Rangers supporters to stand and wave their wallets at Celtic supporters – during the period when the Ibrox side was outspending their rivals – with the roles being reversed in the last three years.

Sectarian offences are now the most likely to result in police action, if supporters resort to calling each other 'Fenians' or 'dirty Orange bastards'. Overtly aggressive behaviour – sustained abuse, physical gestures, tirades – are also acted upon. 'That is crossing the line,' Mawson says, 'because it's not just about the people wanting to get involved in that kind of stuff. We have to remember that it's a family sporting event and not fifty yards away there will be adults and children at the game together. When that rare behaviour happens, you have to take robust action.'

During the interval, which lasts precisely fifteen minutes, Mawson sends teams of officers to known trouble spots inside the stadium concourse, and to assist stewards in maintaining the no-smoking ban. After the second half kicks off, Rangers supporters break into a rendition of 'Follow Follow'; then, to the tune of 'The Billy Boys', chant Maurice Edu's name over and over again. Banners are raised, flags lifted, scarves brandished, and voices unleashed. Mawson looks on.

The Scottish Cup final of 10 May 1980 lacks decisive moments and drifts, tensely, into extra time. Hampden Park is crammed with 70,303 supporters, and a dry, dense heat hangs over the old stadium, wisps of dust swirling in the balmy summer wind. It is almost a glum occasion, and the order is passed for police officers inside the ground to leave and prepare to assist colleagues in patrolling the crowds as they head home. By the time the game finishes, only eight police officers can be seen at the Celtic end of the ground.

On the terraces, cans of beer – many of them the Tennent's brand bearing models in their underwear – are drained then tossed towards the pitch. Most spray beer over the crowd before landing on the heads of fellow supporters at the front of the stand. Throughout the game, men have been pulling carry-outs from beneath the wide flares of their jeans: lager cans, bottles of Pomagne cider and whisky. The stone steps of the terraces are sticky and cluttered with crushed cans and broken bottles. After major games, it often takes ten industrial skips to clear all the debris from stadiums.

The Celtic captain on the day is Danny McGrain, the accomplished Scotland full-back who grew up a Protestant and a committed Rangers supporter (it is often alleged he was ignored by Ibrox scouts because his surname seemed Catholic). By the start of the second period of extra time, he is exhausted, drained of everything but the will to keep moving. When the ball breaks to him from the Rangers penalty area, he can reach only for the strength to swing his right foot at it. The shot is sclaffed, as the ball bounces off his shin before making contact with his foot, and is heading sorrowfully wide. Then George McCluskey, the Celtic striker, sticks out his leg to divert the ball past Peter McCloy, the Rangers goalkeeper: 1–0.

Rangers cannot summon the vigour to respond. Outside the ground, the vast majority of the 400 to 500 police officers on duty at the game are ready to usher the supporters home. Local residents have become increasingly exasperated by the fighting, the urinating in gardens, the loutishness and the general waft of chaos that follows matches at the national stadium, and the intention is to lead supporters away from Hampden and disperse the crowds with as little disruption as possible. When the final whistle blows, the Rangers team quickly heads up the tunnel, while the Celtic players, exhausted but beaming, trudge towards the end of the ground containing their fans to celebrate.

A six-foot high perimeter fence runs right along the front of the terracing, penning the supporters in, but it is easily scaled (on the morning of the game, a steward showed how it was possible to climb over the fence in fifteen seconds). A few exuberant young Celtic supporters haul themselves over to dart onto the pitch among the players and celebrate the moment. It is little more than a mischievous act, but then some adults follow. At the other side of the ground, Rangers fans are slowly beginning to leave, and growing increasingly resentful towards the scene at the Celtic end. Then a supporter crosses the halfway line, runs towards the Rangers end and makes a gesture – partly defiant, partly aggressive. It is enough to provoke a reaction. 'Fuckin' bastard. I'll have you.' And it spreads rapidly through the Rangers fans, gathering momentum and urgency.

Archie MacPherson is in the television gantry, where he is commentating live on the game. 'They're spilling right onto the pitch,' he says in a frantic voice. 'And where are the police? For heaven's sake, where are the police?' Within moments, the pitch is inundated with around 1,000 supporters charging at each other, their feet obscured by the flares of their trousers, wearing tank tops and t-shirts, with clumps of long curly hair flapping, and scarves, tied to their wrists, billowing through the air. Punches are thrown as rival fans collide. Kicks are aimed with viciousness but they are also haphazard, since so many of the supporters are drunk. Blows are often misplaced but some supporters are hurling bricks and bottles. In the midst of the battles, shouts and grunts can be heard, but the predominant sound is the swish of hurled lager cans cutting through the air.

Little more than a dozen police officers, some with batons, are on the pitch, wrestling with supporters, and all of them thinking, where the hell is everybody else, where are our colleagues? There is bedlam as everybody fights each other, and injured fans, many with blood pouring from head wounds, are tended to by dazed friends and dragged towards the penalty areas at either side of the pitch. 'This is like a scene out of *Apocalypse Now*,' says MacPherson to the nation. 'We've got the equivalent of Passchendaele and that says nothing for Scottish football. Let's not kid ourselves. These supporters hate each other.'

Outside, mounted police are waiting in the heat of the late afternoon sun, their horses sweating and moving restlessly. They include Elaine Mudie, a 22-year-old WPC, and her horse, Ballantrae. The police radios begin to hiss with sharp, pleading cries for help. An order is issued for the officers to raise their batons, the first time this has happened since the General Strike in 1926, and to return to the inside of the stadium immediately.

The Celtic players are back in their dressing room, many of them oblivious to the carnage on the pitch. As the Rangers team walk up the main stand to collect their losers' medals, they look down on the fighting, incredulous. Then a dull roar can be heard as mounted police appear at the Celtic end of the ground. The hooves of the galloping horses thud forcefully on the grass pitch. Mudie is scared as she steers her grey gelding towards the fans, while trying to evade the flying bottles, cans and bricks. She is the first female mountie to be involved in such a charge in Britain, and the intervention seems symbolic. Of all the dozen or so police horses involved, hers is the lightest in colour, so the most conspicuous, and the supporters quickly begin to scatter back towards the terraces.

A *Daily Record* photographer, Eric Craig, is trying to capture the havoc of the riot as the mounted officers hurtle into the crowd. He is oblivious as a half-empty bottle of Pomagne, seemingly thrown from the Rangers end, cracks into the back of his skull, causing a depressed fracture. It takes a six-hour emergency brain operation at the neurosurgical unit of the Southern General Hospital to repair the damage, and he is left partially deaf in his right ear. As order is restored, Mudie turns her horse back towards the exit. When she passes the main stand, the remaining supporters rise to applaud her; she begins to cry, partly in gratitude, but mostly in relief.

The green turf of the Hampden pitch is pockmarked with broken bottles, stones and cans, as well as scarves, jackets and other pieces of clothing torn off in the mayhem. It is a grim, dirty mess. Having changed quickly, the Rangers players are on the coach and driving away from the ground. A second bus carrying their wives and girl-friends is travelling behind them, but is caught by a group of Celtic fans and roughly shaken.

Accusations are traded in the aftermath, with the incident debated in the House of Commons. The police blame the Celtic players for celebrating, and the Celtic supporters for invading the pitch. Celtic blame the police for not managing the situation, and sectarianism among the Rangers fans who took to the field looking for a fight. 'Although I only checked on the details later, I can tell you that Celtic's cup final side featured six Catholic players and five Protes-tants, who include our captain, Danny McGrain,' says Desmond White, the Celtic chairman. The Scottish Football Association say the police were at fault, and fine both clubs £20,000.

In all, the riot results in 100 casualties – including 4 police officers – with 50 people requiring hospital treatment, and a total of 210 arrests, 160 of which were made inside the ground. The ultimate response is the Criminal Justice (Scotland) Bill, which introduces a complete ban on alcohol at all football grounds in the country.

The time is now 2 p.m., and the attention in the control room is on preparing for the end of the game, which has only fifteen minutes left to play, and then the aftermath. 'Send up the helicopter,' Mawson instructs. Once airborne, the police chopper will feed live video footage to the heli-telly downlink, providing coverage of the entire area around Celtic Park. The outer perimeter of the stadium is also monitored by fixed CCTV cameras, as supporters can walk round the entire ground unhindered – when they leave they can, in theory, depart in any direction.

'Put the barriers up,' Mawson then orders. The junction with Springfield Road and London Road is a potential flashpoint for fans, and so eight-feet-high solid metal barriers are erected across the street and down London Road, which filters Rangers fans in one direction and Celtic fans in the other. The barriers are brutally solid and intimidating, and the two sets of supporters cannot even see each other, which in turn prevents much of their singing and swapping of abuse.

According to The Log, it is time to monitor the crowd densities, identifying which stadium exits need to be opened and when. Some supporters start to leave before the end of the game, then a surge follows the final whistle, with the stadium cleared within minutes. Mawson is also watching for potential conflicts, or rival gangs coming together, particularly outside the ground. The heli-telly link allows him access to this area and, in combination with the CCTV coverage inside the stadium, he oversees the entire dispersal of the crowd. The room is still a thrum of concentrated activity, audio and visual information being constantly relayed. The atmosphere is different to a normal game, more brooding; every decision is potentially fateful.

The control room remains manned for half an hour after the final whistle. The stadium empties rapidly, and the Rangers fans leave at the same time as the home support, because the routes to and from the ground are distinct for the two sets of supporters, and they are kept apart. The fixed CCTV cameras, the heli-telly and officers spread around the area keep Mawson informed of the flow of people away from Celtic Park. It soon becomes an eerie scene outside the control room, the stands empty apart from stewards checking each row of seats. It is calm inside the room, but there is still an air of vigilance. Once the area around Celtic Park has returned to normal, Mawson contacts the chief superintendent at Govan police station. 'Right, I'm standing down the match. It's all yours.'

Almost eighteen months ago, Strathclyde Police introduced a new system for maintaining order on Old Firm days, treating them as force-wide events. As well as a match commander taking charge of events at Celtic Park and the immediate surroundings, a second chief superintendent is in place at the area control room in Govan police station, taking command of the entire Strathclyde Police force. This is a bigger room, with more officers and more banks of CCTV screens. Footage is relayed from throughout Glasgow city centre, and beyond if reports of disorder are received, and particular attention is paid to known trouble spots, or to the outside of pubs that always attract large numbers of Old Firm fans.

This second chief superintendent can deploy officers anywhere in the region. Glasgow is an obvious danger zone for supporters encountering rivals group as they make their way home from the match, and policing is stepped up at all the major train and bus stations, as well as the city centre itself. The suburbs are also closely monitored, as people will often watch the match in their local pub then carry on drinking for the rest of the afternoon before heading home, causing the potential for skirmishes late into the evening. Forces outwith Strathclyde are also on alert, as disturbances have been known to break out as far away as Edinburgh, Inverness and Ayrshire.

Around nine o'clock in the evening, the area command room at Govan returns to normal and the second chief superintendent relinquishes control of the entire force. Having returned to London Road police station after the match, then held a hot debrief with his command team of inspectors, chief inspectors and above to review and update and improve The Plan and The Log for the next Old Firm encounter, Mawson is completing the last of his paperwork.

Only half a dozen arrests were made at the stadium, mostly for alcohol-related incidents. On this occasion, the level of violence inside and around the ground was minimal and few supporters will have felt genuinely threatened. It has been a typical Old Firm occasion – tense, occasionally unhinged, but always under control.

'It's a nice feeling when it's gone well, the arrests are minimal and you've got everybody in safely, no one's got injured, they've enjoyed the game and they've got home safely,' Mawson says. 'At the game, the violence was low, arrests were low, and across the city trouble was low; it was really well managed. That's a good day.'

By 10 p.m., Wayne Mawson is finally able to head for home.

CHAPTER 6
THE COVERAGE

'Let's look at the men who matter on derby day in Glasgow. Celtic make two changes from the Hamilton game on Boxing Day and two big players drop to the bench: top scorer Scott McDonald and skipper Stephen McManus. Gary Caldwell is back from a ban and there is an Old Firm initiation for Marc-Antoine Fortune. Danny Fox makes his derby debut, too. Rangers make two changes from the side that hammered Dundee United. Kenny Miller is suspended after his red card in that game, Madjid Bougherra has gone to the African Nations Cup. There's a first taste of the Old Firm experience for eighteen-year-old Danny Wilson, and Steven Whittaker returns to the side. It's Kris Boyd's first start at Celtic Park for three and a half years. For any lingering New Year hangovers, this should do the trick. It's the wake-up call to beat them all: an Old Firm game.

'Steve Conroy takes charge of an Old Firm game for the very first time. Good luck to him. He sent off Walter Smith and Pedro Mendes at Kilmarnock earlier in the season. It's not quite a high noon shoot-out, but what's half an hour between enemies? The fans of Celtic and Rangers will be hoping for the best and fearing the worst, but that's football for you. The only sure thing is that it's going to be totally unpredictable.'

Ian Crocker, the Sky commentator, has been up since 7 a.m. He's spent the morning reading all of the newspapers to keep up to date with the backstories and disputes shaping this latest encounter, and running through in his head some phrases he will use before the game kicks off (he says nothing at the particular moment the game begins, preferring to let the noise from the crowd within the stadium be the accompaniment to the pictures). A little before 9 a.m., Crocker phones Walter Smith, the Rangers manager, for news of the starting line-up and the formation, which he then passes on to Sky Sport's graphics team, who are sworn to secrecy. Under Tony Mowbray and Gordon Strachan, Celtic have been less forthcoming about their team, although Martin O'Neill used to be more willing to share his thoughts on the formation at least, and would often shove a crumpled piece of paper into Crocker's hand before kick-off with the formation written down. Crocker arrives at the stadium three hours before the game is due to begin, when supporters are already milling around outside, something uncommon at most other grounds. Then half an hour before kick-off, he heads for the gantry at Celtic Park, which involves walking up hundreds of steps to the back of the main stand, then up and over the roof. Sometimes, Crocker slides forward to the very edge to peer over onto the seats and pitch below – a sweeping view that takes in the building anticipation, the sense of something momentous about the occur – then scurries down a ladder to the television gantry.

'I never believe any manager who says they don't read the papers or listen to a word commentators say. One Old Firm manager used to say that all the time, yet was soon on the phone to me one Monday morning to complain,' says Crocker. 'All commentators aim to build a relationship with managers. If I don't know a manager, I will try to watch his team or go to see them train, where managers are more relaxed. Once you've established trust, you'd be ringing the managers on a match day for an early shout on the teams. TV commentators are obsessed with getting teams early, not just to help ourselves but also the production people getting the fancy team graphics together that appear on screen before kick-off. At the moment, eleven of the twelve SPL managers will help me with a shout on their team. I'll take that ratio happily. When I covered the Championship in England, twenty-two out of twenty-four managers would tell me their team; I was quite proud of that. And in twenty-one years of commentating on radio and TV, I've only ever fallen out with one manager who wasn't happy about some minor comment I'd made. That was in Glasgow though . . . I guess it just had to be.'

The noise is so loud at Old Firm games that the engineers have to turn up the fader that mixes out the sound of the crowd in the commentator's headphones. As he prepares to begin his commentary, Crocker runs through some of the background work he has carried out on the players, the context of this particular game, and a little bit of history, anything to avoid thinking about the size and reach of the audience he is broadcasting to. The media coverage during the build-up to the game has centered on Tony Mowbray, a Celtic manager already beginning to look haunted. In the five months of the season, his team has performed unconvincingly, and in particular conceded sloppy goals – most evocatively at Ibrox earlier in the campaign, when the Rangers striker Kenny Miller twice surged past the Celtic centre-backs before scoring. Mowbray has come to look flawed, but also helpless. Celtic have lost three league games already, been knocked out of the League Cup by Hearts and suffered indifferent results in the Europa League. In the media, particularly the newspapers, Mowbray is becoming a diminished figure, and vulnerable. Once an individual becomes so undermined, the criticism, and at times the derision, becomes self-fulfilling. Both John Barnes, at Celtic, and Paul Le Guen, at Rangers, did not last a full season because results left them exposed to the biting criticisms of the media, and when a manager is depicted as being hapless, as George Burley and Berti Vogts found during their time in charge of the Scotland national team, there is little chance of redemption. The media can be ruthless in its rejection of a manager.

The language of sports writing is increasingly vehement, and the judgements remorseless. But then football, particularly a rivalry like Celtic v. Rangers, responds to this kind of excessive coverage. The hype can seem overwhelming, but for the clubs and the television companies it brings with it a priceless level of publicity.

'I often marvel as I look around the stadium as the match kicks off, taking in the colour, the atmosphere, the raucous noise and the sense of anticipation, and it is at times quite overwhelming,' says Richard Gordon, who presents BBC Radio Scotland's *Sportsound* programme, which broadcasts the games live. 'But when you listen carefully to some of the songs being sung and hear the hatred spewing from the stands, then it is overwhelming in an entirely different way. They are an absolute assault on the senses in so many ways; they do excite me, and they quite often leave me feeling drained. The first one I attended was in March 1992, the Scottish Cup semi-final which Rangers won 1–0 despite having David Robertson sent off early on. It was before Hampden had been redeveloped and I remember handing over to the commentary team then opening the small hatch window in our box and sticking my head out. The wall of noise completely blew me away.'

The relationship between the media and the Old Firm is double-edged. Journalists need access to players and managers to fill the increasing number of pages that are devoted to both clubs. Most of the indigenous newspapers, and the UK titles that maintain Scottish editions, will carry at least one Rangers and Celtic story every day, because that is what sells copies; fans of the two clubs crave information, and so the newspapers jostle for the best coverage, the best access. This is in the clubs' control, because permission has to be sought for every interview, even if arranged already with the individual, and they use this position to their advantage. When either team wants a particular initiative publicised, or if ticket sales need a boost in the run-up to games, they call a press conference knowing that they will then be guaranteed several pages of coverage in every newspaper the following day, often with radio or television broadcasts, or stories on the websites of every newspaper, as well as those of STV, BBC, Radio Clyde and Real Radio. Every scrap of news or information is pored over, and analysis of the state of both clubs is constant.

In recent years, as well as the rise in newspaper reporting of the Old Firm – Scotland has six national newspapers of its own, and eight UK titles with Scottish offices – and the expanding television coverage – both Sky and ESPN broadcast live matches, while BBC Scotland produces a highlights show – three national radio stations produce football content every weeknight. On Radio Clyde and Real Radio, this takes the form of phone-in shows, where members of the public air their views, which are responded to, or provoked, by a panel of broadcasters, often including a journalist and a former player or manager. It is shows like these, as well as the *Daily Record*'s Hotline (which invites supporters to phone in to make comments that appear in the following day's newspaper) and supporters' internet sites such as FollowFollow and Kerrydale Street, that allow opinions and stories to proliferate. A rumour can race through Glasgow, and the city is so in thrall to the Old Firm that the chatter about Celtic and Rangers seems constant.

Mowbray's position is made harder by his portrayal as a manager under pressure who is sensitive to the way his team is assessed. This coverage is mainly influenced by results, but also his air of exasperation and the way he lacks the stern authority of his Rangers counterpart, Walter Smith. In the rivalry of the Old Firm, everything is seen as a contrast between the two clubs, and the Ibrox manager is a more formidable figure; he possesses a natural command, having known most of the journalists and broadcasters for many years. Through experience he has a gained better grasp of the media, how it works and the demands that it makes, and he enjoys the perspective of an experienced manager, one who is comfortable with his achievements and approach, who is not striving to make his name. The two men are opposites, with Smith currently seen as strong and dynamic (even though he has known the wrath of critical headlines and supporter frustration). Mowbray has been the main subject ahead of this game; it is his reign that is under close scrutiny, it is his signings – Marc-Antoine Fortune, Landry N'Guemo and Danny Fox – who have yet to impress, and the major story would be a Celtic defeat.

In a small changing room at Celtic's training ground in Lennoxtown days before the game, a cold, featureless space containing only a table and chairs and surrounded by a bench running along the walls, the journalists sit waiting for Mowbray. 'Well, what will we ask him today?' someone says with a wry smile. The Celtic job seems to have changed Mowbray, from the engaging, charismatic manager he was at Hibernian four years before, to a careworn figure, his face creased. There is no need to discuss a line of enquiry when Mowbray himself is so clearly the story. The journalists all know each other and there is an easy amiability to the small talk that fills the time, most of which centres on how long it is taking for the Celtic manager to appear. A reporter's life is mostly spent waiting, then being brushed off, so a ready cynicism becomes their default air. The more assertive personalities dominate the conversation, but there is no sense of direct competition; instead, anecdotes are told about the misfortunes or absurdity of other colleagues' behaviour or work. Because Mowbray is wearied rather than riled by the press, there is no sense of anticipation. Gordon Strachan was so unpredictable – and often confrontational – that his conferences could be tense occasions, while

Graeme Souness had several reporters banned during his time in charge of Rangers. Martin O'Neill was an evasive but loquacious interviewee, although he could occasionally become exasperated, and reporters tended to leave his press conferences feeling as though they had learned something worthwhile about some subject or other (and not always football, or Celtic).

When Mowbray eventually walks in and sits down, the journalists all push their dictaphones towards him in expectation. He is a tall, broad man, a mighty and blunt defender in his playing days, but now less intimidating in his training gear and his solemnity, exuding an air of weariness. His dark eyes are sombre, as if holding within them a great regret, and he dismisses an opening question about Christmas Day: 'The kids opened presents, I played with them . . .' A press officer sits nearby on the bench that runs beneath the changing pegs, looking at the ground while listening to the question and answer session; it is never hostile but he is in no doubt about the story of this impending Old Firm game: Mowbray himself, so it feels like an interrogation, and the questions come one after each other, with the more domineering figures asking more, but everybody taking their turn. Tabloid reporters are a little more blunt as they seek a news-line strong enough to make the back page, while broadsheet journalists can be more indulgent and contrary, but the overriding theme is the same: Mowbray is being probed.

Any concerns about the defence, Tony?

'I don't see a major problem with the defenders themselves having fears. If you allow it to get on top of you, then it is a problem. The central defenders are very experienced players who understand their jobs. They need to concentrate, be focused and do what they do best. There will be no problems, I am sure.'

Do you enjoy the Old Firm game?

'I was quoted the other week as saying you don't enjoy the job anyway – it's just the next game for me. It'll have a psychological effect on the team, either positively or negatively; when the game after that comes along, you either have to pick them up or keep their feet on the ground.'

Is there still an aura around an Old Firm game then?

'For players and managers, it genuinely is about the three points. It is a cliché, but sometimes clichés are right. No one's trying to diminish how big an event it is – the fact you can't get a ticket tells you the passion will be there on the terrace. But there are only three points at stake and nothing will be defined on the back of it. If the worst came to the worst and we didn't win on Sunday, there's nothing won or lost, and we can keep going to try to find the consistency to win points.'

How do you address your strikers' shots-to-goal ratio?

'If you watched us train, you'd see us put them in scenarios where they hit the net as often as possible. You overload training, four attackers against two defenders, and you hope they work to use the spare men and they score and get their confidence levels up. That's what football is, practising good habits and preaching the right techniques so they go into matches confident [and] when it falls to them in the box in the hurly burly of an Old Firm game, 60,000 people chanting, they just go cold and pass it into the corner, like they've done a million times before. That's what the best strikers do – it's instinct.'

Are you tempted to change the team shape or your selections?

'Not for me. I spend a lot of time trying to bed down the players on how we play, and if your systems and your shapes work well enough, however well the opposition knows them, you can still give them problems. So play to your own strengths and don't worry about them. Otherwise, if you get over concerned about the opposition you'll lose focus on what you're trying to do yourself.'

Will the physicality of Rangers, or the need to fill the midfield, be a factor?

'That's almost a leading question, because if I say, "No, we'll just got out and play", and we get beaten, you're naïve. I've been there last year in the Premier League [as West Brom manager]. It could be that we dominated the game, we had total control, we missed loads of chances and hit the bar four or five times, but we got beaten 1–0 and you're naïve because you didn't play five in midfield. If it was blatantly in your face that we were getting overrun and over-powered in midfield I'd have to hold my hand up and say I got it wrong. But if your wide players are killing them because they've got no protection out there – just three in midfield and their two wide players aren't tracking back – and McGeady is skating past their defender every time and making chance after chance after chance but they score from a corner, no one's interested. They're only inter-ested in, "God, he's naïve – he didn't play three in midfield to match their three." Am I going to stiffen up the midfield? I don't know. I don't think so. I know you can't see the bigger picture sometimes, so even if we go to Hearts and we lose 2–1 – you probably wrote it up negatively as poor Celtic, naïve Celtic – but if you love football and you watch the game, we created lots of chances, we should have won. You've got to write negatively. It's your jobs, I suppose, but I as a coach think, "You're not wrong, keep doing what you believe in because that's going to get you success."'

He sounds like a manager reduced to self-justification, and his responses are pored over for indications as to his state of mind, his confidence, and for how this Old Firm game might play out. In his answers, about the virtues of his approach, about the nega-tivity that is not only written but expected in the newspapers, he betrays his sense of being pilloried. He is attempting defiance, but it comes across as disdain. On this Sunday afternoon at Celtic Park, Mowbray will stand on the touchline, isolated, and the watching media will present the outcome in the way that it affects him: a Celtic win means that he has reasserted himself and that the team, his idealism, is still valid; a Celtic defeat and he will be a man on the brink. Hero or villain; there is no middle-ground.

'Kick-off. Football in 2010 starts with a bang, and it's the loudest of bangs: Celtic against Rangers, and Lafferty goes up with Robson straight away. Samaras and Weir going for that, but it's Broadfoot who's able to steer it back to McGregor. The first goal is crucial in every game, but especially this one. Only once in the last sixty-three league derbies has the team scoring first lost.

'He's [Boruc] a man for these occasions, he's certainly rubbed the Rangers fans up the wrong way a few times.

'Nacho Novo, who has been feeling a little ill this week, but he wasn't going to miss out on a trip to the arch enemy. He's got a good record in these games.

'The majority inside Celtic Park would dearly love an early opener for the men in hoops, to set the tone, to set their stall out.

'Tony Mowbray lost his first Old Firm game as a manager; he did win three as a player, and scored in one of them in fact, on his Old Firm debut. The managers really are under intense pressure and a bright spotlight on days like this, especially Mowbray, who has found the going a little tough so far in the Glasgow goldfish bowl.

'Crosas . . . Samaras . . . he was going to get a free kick eventually and he has. Caldwell and Loovens will join Samaras and Fortune in there. Will this be a key moment for Celtic? Robson takes it, McGeady . . . he didn't really connect, but McGregor was put under pressure . . . and fouled. Was he? The referee has pulled it back, it is a free kick. I don't think his assistant referee gave that either, it was Steve Conroy's decision, and he got it wrong. Allan McGregor, with a huge let off there. Steve Conroy's first Old Firm *game and that was a huge decision, a decision that certainly favoured Rangers. Celtic will be bemused why Fortune's goal didn't stand.*

'This first half is flying by, as per usual. It's the kind of day when nothing less than total commitment counts. You have to give your all, or you'll soon be found out; no hiding place when the giants of Glasgow collide.

'Kyle Lafferty may well be getting a yellow card for that challenge, he's left Hinkel in a heap. He is one lucky boy Kyle Lafferty, that is for sure. Thankfully Hinkel's not too badly hurt, but it could easily have been a red. Shocker of a tackle from Lafferty. Lafferty jeered now by the Celtic fans. A potential leg breaker.

'Crosas . . . and Broadfoot nudging it away, but McGeady's kept it in, he's not let that go for the corner. No respite for Rangers, away by McCulloch. N'Guemo feeding Hinkel, promising this, Robson . . . it bounces off the bar from Barry Robson.

'Well, they've had a goal harshly disallowed and they've hit the bar. They're dominant as far as attempts on goal are concerned. Nothing on target yet for Rangers, nothing much happening at all. It's Walter Smith's forty-seventh Old Firm game, he's only lost eleven, a remarkable record in Glasgow derbies. It's a fairly new experience, in contrast, for Tony Mowbray. Rangers have barely had a shot in anger, but strange things can happen on derby day in Glasgow.

'Fortune . . . Crosas . . . stray pass from the boy from Barcelona, which is unlike him. He's won it back now, though. Fortune ran into Weir, Samaras takes over, he's in, and he's put it wide. What a miss from Georgios Samaras.

'With half time fast approaching it remains goalless, and Celtic will wonder how. The forty-five minutes are almost up. Celtic have been in charge of this Old Firm game – can they end the half on a high, the highest of highs, taking the lead against their fierce

rivals? We're into two minutes of stoppage time. Robson takes it, Samaras let it drop . . . wanted to do too much, I think.

'Tony Mowbray will be concerned that his side haven't made their pressure pay; Walter Smith slightly relieved at the moment, because Rangers have offered little. But most games in football can change quickly, and this one certainly can. Who knows what awaits us in the second half on derby day in Glasgow? That's it, half time. There's been a few big incidents, though none bigger than Marc-Antoine Fortune's disallowed goal; Georgios Samaras was through on goal but squandered his opportunity. Kyle Lafferty got a yellow when he might have got a red. It's been fairly fast and fairly frantic – we expect nothing else – but at half time it's Celtic 0, Rangers 0.'

In the Celtic Park media room at half time, journalists gather around the solitary television set, a small, square screen that is mounted high up in the far corner. On two of the walls, framed Celtic jerseys from throughout the club's history have been hung, but otherwise it is a room without character, reduced only to a crowded working space. There is a bustling murmur as incidents are discussed; some voices are projected louder than the others in a show of bravado, then the replays are broadcast in the television coverage. The mood is one of frantic collaboration, as incidents are discussed and opinions shared. The footage shows Fortune making contact with McGregor's arm as he jumped to head the ball past the Celtic goalkeeper, and opinion is divided about the referee's decision to disallow the goal, although most decide that the referee was too harsh. The views are not wholly split along the lines of which of the two teams some of the journalists support, since the obligation at this stage is to be true to the story rather than individual allegiances. When Kyle Lafferty's challenge on Andreas Hinkel comes on, there is a sharp intake of breath as the Rangers striker's studs land midway up the Celtic defender's lower leg and the camera catches Mowbray turning away on the touchline, his jacket flapping behind him, both hands planted on top of his head and an agonised look on his face. It becomes one of the images of the day; a snapshot of the game's uncompromising nature, of its recklessness, but also of Mowbray, wincing and unnerved, having to shy away from it.

Judgements have already been made by the radio and television commentators, whose coverage is live, but the footage hardens the viewpoints taken by the newspaper journalists, whose match reports are written during the game and filed almost immediately after the final whistle, so that second and third pieces can be written using the quotes of the managers and the players. Most newspapers have at least three reporters at the game, and many will have between six and fourteen pages of Old Firm coverage to fill. The reporting, the analysis, is incessant. Radio Scotland is broadcasting the game live, as is Sky, and both have teams of technicians, presenters, reporters and expert pundits – former Old Firm players like Davie Provan, Charlie Nicholas, Neil McCann and Murdo McLeod – all picking over the details of the game, adding to the clamour with their own critical voices.

For journalists, the Old Firm clubs dominate because of the vast size of their support, but also because they are Scottish institutions, and newsworthy in a way that other teams are not. A study in 2005 estimated that the Old Firm clubs are worth £120 million to the Scottish economy annually and create thousands of jobs for the country, with the figures including money spent by supporters at games, as well as travel, food and drink, and the impact on the hospitality industry.

The religious nature of the rivalry means that stories about the two teams, however detached they might be from the football itself, can be sensationalised. It is not unusual for an Old Firm footballer to appear on the front pages of the tabloid newspapers because of some drama in their private life – Allan McGregor, the Rangers goalkeeper, and Artur Boruc, his Celtic counterpart, have both seen stories about their romantic lives covered in the newspapers, while Kyle Lafferty, the Rangers striker, was reported to have parked his car in a disabled space, prompting an outraged news report. There is no story too small. So in the run up to this game, one newspaper carried a feature under the headline, 'Old Firm Battle Of The Babes; Which Sexy Celebs Back Footie Giants?', which revealed that Penny Lancaster, Martine McCutcheon, Nadine Coyle and Shirley Manson all support Celtic, while Nell McAndrew, Carol Smillie, Suzanne Carlsson and Amy Macdonald all follow Rangers. These are trivialities, but they still feed into the obsession around the two clubs in the same way as measured and thought-provoking opinion pieces in the comment pages of the broadsheet newspapers, even if it is to a lesser extent than the coverage that followed Boruc being charged by police after blessing himself during an Old Firm game, or the furore that followed the 1980 Scottish Cup final riot. Coverage of Celtic and Rangers often becomes social or political commentary because of their background, in a way that even clubs the size of Manchester United, Arsenal and Liverpool do not encounter.

'Twenty years spans the time period during which I have attended these games, and the Old Firm game has become a more significant occasion, partly because of the additional media build-up and guaranteed live TV coverage, and partly because since the late eighties, early nineties the race for the title has once again become a two-horse race, with the encounters between the two sides so often decisive,' says Richard Gordon. 'Coverage is probably more sensationalist, but reporting in general has headed in that direction over the past couple of decades, so that reflects the general trend. I don't think this has any real impact on the fixture itself as those involved, whether as players, management or fans, are all well aware of the importance of the game. I don't believe that media coverage affects the intensity in the slightest beforehand or after, although those who are emotionally involved in the fixture would probably beg to differ. There are always plenty of fans on either side of the divide who are determined to find a bias in the coverage – they will do that irrespective of whether it exists or not.'

The language of the coverage tends to be aggressive; reports talk about battles, fight, heart, spirit, courage. Sports writing has often invoked war imagery because it is the confrontational aspect that is so vital to the grip that sport has on people. In the UK, football coverage tends to rush into hyperbole, into tales of triumph and tragedy, into the *Super Sunday* extravaganzas that Sky Sports promote so breathlessly; there is such a weight of significance placed on crucial fixtures that the games and the reporting of them become charged. Because the Old Firm matches can have social consequences – in combination with the heavy drinking that is prevalent in the west of Scotland, assaults, domestic violence and accident and emergency attendances all rise after matches – they are further magnified, and so a self-perpetuating cycle is established: the media generate hype around the game, which fuels the intensity of a match already pressurised by the age-old rivalry between the two sets of supporters. It is not uncommon for previous Old Firm battles or flashpoints to be recounted in the build-up to games, but then newspaper, television and radio coverage will quickly condemn any further altercations if they occur. It is gleeful, this revelling in past indiscretions, before new ones are denounced and moralised over.

It is also a double-edged relationship for both the media and the footballers. They are all are obliged to take part in press conferences, even if the player has no wish to be there and his answers are so mundane that the journalists do not wish to be there, either. Footballers often tend to be defensive, because they have seen unguarded or ill-advised comments turned into headlines. So rather than be sure of themselves and their point of view, they opt to be withdrawn and reluctant. There also tends to be a difference in age and maturity, since many footballers are in their early twenties or late teens, still gauche and unknowing, while the journalists are in their thirties or older, hardened, sharpened. Yet both need each other to exist, to make the most of their relationship: publicity for the clubs, access for the media. Until around the mid-1980s, it was common for reporters and footballers to be friends, to socialise together away from the set-piece meetings of their working lives, safe in the knowledge that the exploits of either – drinking, sexual, or the kind of boisterousness that young men easily fall into – would never be known outwith their circle. But that was a time when sport took up only two or three pages of newspapers, mostly containing drily factual match reports or news stories concerning injuries. Footballers then were paid similar wages to supporters, and celebrity was a rare, unfamiliar concept; now, the demand is for drama and 'colour', for stories and interviews that carry an impact, and all the better if there is a confrontational edge, while the game is no longer low-key and localised.

'The chance to build relationships with Old Firm players is much reduced from what it was in the early nineties,' says Gordon. 'One-to-one interviews are less frequently available, with players instead put up at staged news conferences where, under the watchful eye of a club PR person, they almost without fail follow the party line and say little of consequence. There is less trust generally between players and the media, and that is as a direct result of us not being able to sit down and get to know them on a personal basis. There are of course exceptions, but in the main they are kept at a distance and that has inevitably affected the way we cover the game from a player's point of view. I do still believe there is a fair degree of respect between the clubs and most of us in the media. I personally have had no problem at all with the management of either Celtic and Rangers, and probably more importantly, the PR and backroom teams at both clubs, with whom I feel I have a strong working relationship. Although I would admit to having read stories at times that do appear provocative simply for the sake of it.'

Sometimes the pressure causes an outburst. During one press conference at Murray Park, Alex McLeish was asked about his future, at a time when Rangers were struggling to compete with Celtic. 'Aye well, I've heard that you'll be out of a job before me,' the manager blurted back angrily to the reporter. McLeish later phoned the journalist to apologise. Strachan, too, made a remark about not being able to understand childbirth because he's not a woman, after being asked a question by a female radio reporter. Neither manager's job was affected, but both Paul Le Guen and Mowbray suffered because, sensing they were weak, the press became merciless, although supporters tend to see bias in the coverage, rather than opportunism.

'I strongly believe that the internet and social media has had a major part to play in the rise in recent seasons of sectarianism, bigotry and undisguised hatred between the fans of both clubs,' says Gordon. 'The extreme views, once private, are now opened to a world-wide audience and have an undoubted effect on the rivalry. I am sure every media organisation gets the same kind of mailbag, but I often leave the studio feeling more than a little depressed having spent hours reading texts and emails dripping with hateful bile. It saddens me that there are people out there who believe that the nonsense they spout passes for reasoned and acceptable comment. I have no doubt that there are some of my media colleagues who support either side and may have at times allowed that to creep into their reporting, but in the main it is utter nonsense. In the wake of an Old Firm game we generally get abuse from both sets of fans for being biased; that I suppose means we probably just about get it right.'

'Well, Rangers may have a seven-point lead at the top of the SPL, but they've certainly been under the cosh here and the major decisions in the game have gone their way. Marc-Antoine Fortune's goal wrongly disallowed, and Kyle Lafferty should have been sent off. Celtic it is who start the second half, they'll be kicking themselves that they aren't already in front in this Old Firm match.

'Flicked on by Lafferty for Boyd . . . and Steven Davis . . . Lafferty . . . it's come off Caldwell for a corner. Rangers needed a sense of purpose in this second half, having barely had a look-in. Davis takes the corner, Caldwell cleared it. Weir tries to rescue it, but Celtic bursting away, only Papac and Edu back for Rangers. Rangers exposed, it's Aiden McGeady . . . and he's put it wide. And the familiar story continues for Celtic.

'Celtic rarely have problems creating chances, but scoring them has been another matter for Tony Mowbray. Plus some dodgy defending at times at the other end this season. Well, in the first five minutes of the second half, Rangers have probably already done more in an attacking sense than they did in the first.

'Edu, terrible mistake from him, and Aiden McGeady . . . big chance . . . not taken again. Celtic are having one of those days in front of goal; they've had a few of them, to be fair, this season.

'Anxious moment for Rangers then . . . Robson's corner, away by Lafferty, McDonald firing it back; Fox, cleverly sets up Robson again, and Robson sends Davis the wrong way, but Lafferty helping out his defence. Here's Hinkel . . . Caldwell . . . McGeady, skipped away from Whittaker, McGeady . . . McDonald . . . Scott McDonald comes off the bench to seize the moment, and it's a magic moment for Celtic. They have the lead in the New Year derby. They are finally rewarded for their excellent exploits today. Scott McDonald's fourth goal in ten Old Firm matches has propelled Celtic back into that title race for sure. Rangers rattled now, and Celtic Park is jumping. It took them a while.

'Who can rescue Rangers, if anyone can? Lafferty's hung in there, it's a corner. Well, typical of Scott McDonald to come on and score. Who will step forward for Rangers? The corner from Davis, and the goal from Lee McCulloch. How about that for a swift response? Rangers are level straight away. He's scored a few like that in his time, that's for sure, but a critical goal for Lee McCulloch, and Rangers respond immediately. Celtic Park has gone a little quiet now. Lee McCulloch was the man who stepped forward for Rangers, who answered the call, and who rallied his team. Just two minutes and twenty-two seconds between the goals. Joy very short lived for Tony Mowbray. And that is typical of the resilience of this Rangers side. A fairly routine goal for Celtic to concede, but that's happened a few times this season.

'A fascinating finale now, the Old Firm locked together at 1–1, which will be fine as far as Rangers are concerned, but Celtic need more out of this contest. McGeady . . . Hinkel . . . Samaras . . . oh, an amazing save by Allan McGregor. It looked so goal-bound by Georgios Samaras. That is one of the saves of the season, maybe the save of the season by Allan McGregor. Incredible. McGregor doing his bit for the Rangers cause.

'It's all over, and it's all square. Scott McDonald came off the bench to put Celtic in front, but their lead lasted less than two and a half minutes. Lee McCulloch's header levelling it for Rangers, but Allan McGregor certainly playing his part with a fantastic save, one that simply took your breath away. And Walter Smith still has a seven-point lead at the top. Quite a few incidents along the way, there always is on Old Firm day, and Celtic had a goal wrongly disallowed in the first half for sure. Eventful, incident-packed, plenty of hustle and bustle, it's ended Celtic 1, Rangers 1.'

The final whistle prompts a surge of activity in the press box as journalists try to send their match reports. There are anxious faces, and curses, as the 3G dongles on their laptops fail at the worst possible moment. 'Every bloody time,' someone curses. 'Have you got a signal? What about you?' Those reporters who are writing quotes pieces gather their stuff together quickly and hurry through the crowd, even though none of the players or managers will appear in the press room for some time. Always, the fear is of missing out. Laptop bags bang into fans, and power cables dangle in midair as they rush from their seats into the corridors of the main stand, then into the press room, past the two Celtic officials who man the door. With the game finishing 1–1, the pair nod pensively to each journalist who passes by, while corporate guests and other VIPs stream from the directors' box into the lounges along the same corridor. The contrast between the fraught and occasionally dishevelled journalists and the smartly dressed fans is stark.

Inside the press room, there is a sense of expectation. Glances are solemn and expressions are stern. The real business begins now, of gathering news-lines, of dissecting the game and picking over its controversial moments. The hope is for an outburst or condemnation from the managers or the players. It is only words that matter now – opinion and attitude. Colleagues talk in hushed tones among themselves, usually individuals who support the same team and so are mulling over the outcome. 'Did you see Mowbray's reaction to the Lafferty challenge,' one reporter says to his friend. 'That said it all. Shocker. Absolute shocker.' Some journalists are open about their support for either of the two Old Firm sides, but others hide it behind a supposed allegiance for a smaller club. Mostly this is out of a desire not to be considered biased by supporters, but their colleagues do not tend to be fooled and know well enough who they follow. Even those whose support for another side is genuine will often favour one Old Firm team over the other, and only a few individuals are truly ambivalent. Yet these personal preferences do not tend to influence journalists' reports, because making judgements based on bias would be obvious, and their reputation would be quickly discredited. Instead, it is often the case that supporters of either Old Firm team are more critical of them, as if to compensate.

More loudly, reporters from the same newspaper sort out who will cover the managers and who will cover the players. The tone is frantic, out of habit more than necessity (deadlines are still far away because of the early kick-off) but also because the adrenalin is now surging. This is their moment – the aftermath – and the confrontations are about to begin. Journalists want strong quotes, preferably involving a row or disagreement, to move the story of the game on. The reporters are not competing with each other, since the story is taking place in front of all of them, so there is a sense of togetherness, but it is limited, since everybody is ultimately looking after themselves.

Radio reporters line up their microphone stands on top of a long table that sits on a raised platform at one end of the room. Rows of chairs face this stage, while television cameras stand at the back, trained in a steady scrutiny. There is an edginess as the wait drags on, partly out of anticipation, but also out of an anxiety to start working. There is, too, the ever-present concern that laptops and their 3G dongles continue to behave erratically at just the wrong moment. At the back of the room stands another table, draped in a white tablecloth and holding an array of drinks, including whisky and beer, which is served by a gentle, thoughtful woman called Jennifer; beneath the curls of her white hair, there is a serene look to her eyes, a sense of having seen all this nervous energy before, and knowing how quickly it is spent. She smiles at everybody and they acknowledge her politely by name.

The significant incidents are clear enough: the Fortune goal that Conroy disallowed; the Lafferty tackle on Hinkel; Scott McDonald being dropped to the bench but coming on to score; Allan McGregor's remarkable save; the fact that Celtic remained true to form and created more chances in the game but failed to take them and were then caught out at the back; and that a depleted Rangers team maintained its seven-point lead at the top. Any one of these might lead to back-page headlines, and so even though the result of the game is news-worthy enough, there are other stories to chase. It is ten minutes after the final whistle and the wait continues for the first manager to emerge, to sit down in this small room and try to control it, because the savvy manager will anticipate the questions that are coming and answer them in such a way as to push the news agenda in the direc-tion he wishes. It is an engagement of sorts, a test of willpower. When Walter Smith walks in, the room falls silent as he takes his seat, glancing warily at the cameras, then looking at the faces in front of him, waiting. The radio reporters ask the first questions, because they are broadcast almost immediately with the manager's answers, while the newspaper journalists look on impatiently. Then the microphones are switched off and the writers take over, many of them glancing at their dictaphones with a flash of anxiety, fearing that they forgot to switch them on or that the batteries have run out.

What did you think of the game, Walter?

'We were a little bit fortunate to get a point. We didn't play nearly as well as we have been doing in recent weeks. It was difficult for us, Celtic are always a difficult team to play against at Celtic Park. So from our own point of view, we're delighted to get a point, but a little bit fortunate in the overall game. Celtic created far more oppor-tunities and imposed themselves on the game. Although Allan McGregor really only had one outstanding save, there were a number of misses that left us with an opportunity to get back into the game, which thankfully we took.'

Did you feel the referee made the right call disallowing Fortune's goal?

'I thought that was a foul. [There is silence, then a cautious laugh from the questioner]. I thought it was a foul; d'you want me to say it wasn't or . . .'

No, no, I just wanted your, eh, thoughts on whether the referee made the right call. Have you seen it in slow-mo?

'Sorry?'

Have you seen a repeat of the disallowed goal?

'No, it doesn't matter about repeats, you don't need to look at repeats. I looked at last week's repeat and it didn't matter, so this one won't matter either. Repeats only go the one way.'

As a manager, how do you balance the fact that you maybe weren't at your best today, but you still got a point, so you've not lost and you've still got your lead intact at the top of the table?

'Well, it was a far better point for us than it was for Celtic at this stage of the season. They'll obviously feel a little bit aggrieved about the way they game went, because they didn't win it.'

How good was Allan McGregor's save at the end from Georgios Samaras?

'It was the one outstanding save of the day. The rest of Celtic's opportunities were missed rather than making him make the save.'

So how much can that mean to you, Walter, if they've had so many chances, but they haven't beaten you? How much can that mean for your title hopes?

'It's always a little bit early in the season. People talk about the number of points that you're ahead in the league. You only have to look at the last couple of seasons, there's been many times that teams have been a good few points in front of another and they've been clawed back. We know we can play better, so we have to put our whole concentration on making sure that's what we do. Thank you, and Happy New Year to you all.'

When Mowbray walks in, a similar hush settles on the room. He looks unresponsive, his face furrowed, and he hunches in his seat, his hands thrust into his trouser pockets.

Tony, is there a feeling of disbelief that you've come away after ninety minutes without getting all three points?

'Erm, disbelief, erm, no, I don't think so. We did enough to maybe warrant the three points, but football is about putting the ball in the net; we managed it once and they managed it once. So there's a disappointment, a frustration, words I've used a fair bit this season.'

What's your view on Fortune's chalked-off goal?

'I don't know, I haven't seen it. People I have been doing interviews with downstairs have been suggesting that there wasn't much of an infringement there, yet the referee saw an infringement and gave a free kick. We abide by that week in, week out.'

Do you feel as if you've lost an opportunity here in the title race; if you can't score goals you're not going to be able to challenge Rangers?

'No, no [he laughs, a derisory sound]. Very evidently we can challenge for the title. You gentlemen sat and watched it, it's there in front of your eyes. We will be okay, I'm sure.'

What was the thinking behind not playing Scott McDonald? Were you surprised by his reaction or was that typical, the way he came on and performed?

'Again, I don't understand your question. Was I surprised by his reaction that he came on and scored a goal? No, he's done it at Falkirk this year, he came off the bench and scored two, you know; Scott should be worried that he's not going to be turned into some guy who [specializes in coming off the bench to score]. Scott's not very happy on the bench, of course, and I understand that. But my job is to pick the team that I think can give Rangers the most problems. I don't think anybody could sit here and say the front two didn't give Rangers lots of problems today. I feel vindicated that the decision about team selection was fine.'

Disappointed with the defending at the equaliser?

'Again, frustrated; Artur didn't make a save today and generally the play was flowing towards the other end. We defended set plays particularly well through the vast majority of the game, but then one moment in the game, there you go, we drop the points.'

Are you disappointed that the referee didn't take stronger action against Kyle Lafferty for the challenge on Andy in the first half?

'I've got no argument with the referee at all. You gentlemen will have watched it back on your monitors, I'm pretty sure you can make your own judgements.'

Are you in the market for defenders?

'We're in the market for quality footballers.'

Have you got enough money?

'Who, me personally?'

No, the board

'I don't know. The board are fully aware of the situation. There are a lot of conversations going on at the moment with various clubs, either to sell players or buy players. And here we are in January and it's feeding season, I would suggest, to yourselves. You keep trying to guess where we're going with it. Okay? Thank you.'

Both managers have been sincere in their appraisals, and careful not to condemn the referee. Mowbray side-stepped the opportunity to shift the focus from himself onto Conroy. But the media has its stories anyway, in Smith's quotes about the disallowed goal and playing down the significance of the result, and in Mowbray's responses to the questions about Scott McDonald and the search for new signings. The urgency begins to drain from the room, and the focus shifts to the player interviews. Lee McCulloch and Aiden McGeady arrive separately for their time in front of the media, and the exchanges are less formal than with the two managers.

Lee, were you surprised that you managed to get out of that game with a point?

'Eh, Celtic had the bulk of possession, for large spells of the game they were the better team. We didn't pass the ball as well as we've done maybe in the last three, four, five weeks, so we let ourselves down in that aspect. But it was great character to come back into the game.'

Did you get a chance to speak to Allan McGregor, did he feel he was impeded by Fortune for the chalked-off goal?

'No . . . I didn't . . . get a chance to speak to him [McCulloch laughs warmly]. I couldn't really see it [and he laughs again].'

Lee, that save from Allan, it was kind of Goram-esque, the way he used to do in Old Firm games.

'It was. It took a deflection, I think, the big man's hit the shot and it's come off my foot. It was a great save; Greegsy's been different class last season and this season. When you've got a guy like that in goals, you're always hoping he can pull off a save like that. It's a good comparison, with Goram.'

To retain the title, how important is it to get through this month without losing any players?

'Well we've not got the biggest of squads as it is. It's obviously very important. I think that's Boydy now missing the next league game [through suspension]. I don't know. Is that right? I just gave you all a story there [he laughs].'

Aiden, what do you think about the disallowed goal? Did the referee's decision affect the outcome of the game?

'You can't really blame the referee for us not winning. We had more than enough chances. I've not seen the goal again. At the time I thought he had given it, but he pulled it back for the foul. I wasn't sure what he gave it for. But I don't really want to go into that. From where I was he seemed to do okay.'

What about Lafferty's challenge on Andreas Hinkel? Did you see that?

'I'd never sit here and advocate players being sent off.'

How much of a concern is it that Celtic had most of the play and created most of the chances, but still didn't win the game?

'If you don't score goals then you won't win titles. We really should have had the game wrapped up by half time. I had a couple of chances myself that I should have done a bit better with, especially the second one. We had the majority of possession and all the chances and I can only really remember Rangers having a couple of shots at goal. Then we create a goal and two minutes later Rangers score an easy goal from a set-piece. It's very frustrating. It felt like a defeat walking into the dressing room.'

Once the interviews are over, the transcriptions are split up. 'I'll do McCulloch,' one reporter says. 'And you do McGeady.' The quotes are then passed around the journalists on memory sticks, as they all grab chairs and start to type away on their keyboards. Some look pensive as they dwell over every sentence, while others breeze through their copy. It is quiet now, but not subdued; the sense is of purpose and a hurried industry. Only the broadcasters – commentators and pundits – are relaxed now, and they watch with curiosity, talking in hushed tones among themselves while swigging out of beer bottles.

Having clambered down from the TV gantry, then listened to the press interviews, Crocker is among the broadcasters gathered at the back of the room. They are talking furtively, out of respect for their colleagues who are frantically writing stories of up to one thousand words in less than half an hour. It is a quiet form of frantic endeavour, but there is still a strain to it; it is as if the game continues to provoke, even long after it is finished. The challenge now is to come up with the words, the imagery and the insight to match the game, to analyse it with an unforgiving eye, because supporters (and players and coaching staff) will pore over the following day's papers and agree or disagree with the judgements that are made.

'You cannot beat the buzz of waking up on Old Firm day,' Crocker says. 'I've done nearly forty of them now and have felt the same about each one: the standout fixture in Scotland by a distance and one of the biggest games in Britain and the world. The 2002 Scottish

Cup Final between the teams was one of the most enthralling games I've ever seen. And likewise, Celtic: 6 Rangers: 2 in Martin O'Neill's first Old Firm game. I still have Rangers and Celtic fans quoting commentary lines from those two games . . . eleven and nine years on. That is very flattering and I love the fact that it still means so much to them. That is proper passion. I sometimes sit on the gantry at Ibrox or Celtic Park with my headphones off, appreciating the noise and atmosphere. Bloody fantastic. It sends a shiver down my spine and pumps me up for the game a little bit more. They are fun games to commentate on because they keep you on your toes for ninety minutes. They are a hundred miles per hour . . . and some. It's a high-profile game and I used to read some of the fans' forums to see if we caught the mood with our commentary. But I soon gave up on that as there wasn't ever much in the way of reason, just general abuse and claims of bias. Although I accept that's part of it all and I certainly don't mind a bit of friendly banter. The missus was dismayed at Rangers fans singing, 'You're just a fat Harry Potter' to me at Aberdeen once. I thought it was funny, original, and they may have had a point. Most fans in England are fascinated by Old Firm games and I was no different. I did my first one in 1998, it finished 0–0 but it still flew by and was incident-packed. I keep telling my mates to try to get to one if they can, because there's nothing quite like it. I've seen a few English derbies and I would say Newcastle v. Sunderland and Birmingham v. Aston Villa get close. But not close enough.'

CHAPTER 7

FOOTBALL, BLOOD AND BANDAGES

In quiet moments, nurses check the medical store cupboards, and take mental notes of any supplies that are a little low. It is not unheard of for A&E departments to run out of stitching kits on the day of an Old Firm game, but also for whole wards to be closed to more patients because they are so inundated with victims. Paramedics, sitting in the cabs of their ambulances, or taking time for a quick cigarette outside, are already braced for the call to come through from the control desk to attend an incident at a pub, in a suburb, or down a city-centre side street. What they encounter and what they need to do is always the same: football colours, blood, bandages. In the wards, doctors are expecting broken bones, glass wounds and stabbings, accompanied by aggression in their patients that quickly begins to flag, then aggrieved defiance, then remorse, or a stunned incomprehension at how their day, of watching the football, has ended here. The understanding, though, is that something will happen – it always does.

Extra staff have been added to the accident and emergency department rota, although many will check the Premier League fixture list in advance to try to ensure that they take the weekend off. In the run-up to the game, a major incident briefing was held, when doctors, nurses, paramedics and admin staff were all reminded that the hours following the match are likely to see an increase in people attending casualty, with injuries resulting from violent assaults or accidents, almost all of which will be influenced by heavy drinking. But in the immediate hours after the final whistle, there is little impact on the A&E department, as supporters often tend to make their way home before going back out to the pub, or because the kick-off was so early in the day that they did not have time to drink much before the game. So it becomes a wait, for the inevitable.

The Royal Infirmary is mostly housed in old, grimy Victorian buildings that stand on the north-east corner of Glasgow, looking over the M8 as it cuts through the city centre and the districts of the east end as it spreads out in a flat, urban sprawl of dilapidation, forlorn warehouses and the small, renewed hope of housing schemes. New extensions have been added to the hospital over the years, but where the brittle stone walls are blackened with age, it still retains an ancient, forbidding air. On the day of an Old Firm game at Celtic Park, the emergency department is braced for an influx of casualties beyond the normal flow of trauma that carries through A&E. The city's Southern General hospital, in Govan, does the same when Old Firm games are held at Ibrox; for cup finals or semi-finals involving the teams at Hampden, both of Glasgow's two major hospitals are prepared for an increase in casualty patients that has been estimated to reach as much as three times the normal attendance, while 999 calls have often risen by a quarter. The emergency services and a further fifteen casualty departments across west central Scotland prepare to be inundated, and all draft in extra staff or cancel leave to cope.

Following one Old Firm match in August 2000, which Celtic won 6–2 at Parkhead, there were two murders, two attempted murders, three serious stabbings, fifteen assaults and sixty-two arrests. A thirty-two-year-old man was slashed in the face as he walked along a street in the city's south side wearing the wrong colour scarf. Another forty-year-old man was knocked down by a car and beaten with sticks and golf clubs as he lay unconscious.

The games early in the season are considered less likely to have an impact on hospital admissions, but a fixture at New Year, or games when the Championship race has begun to move towards an inevitable outcome, provoke a greater tension. There are no certainties, though, other than the knowledge that casualties relating in some way to the Old Firm game will arrive, and that excessive drinking will have influenced the injuries. As well as reducing tolerance, alcohol also tends to make people express themselves more physically, as if a violent response is the only way to assert their point of view.

'An Old Firm game creates its own sense of anticipation,' says Dr Michael Sheridan, an A&E consultant at the Royal Infirmary. 'Historically, there's been a bit of concern that Old Firm matches in particular are associated with violence and drink-related attendances. Nowadays, that's not been shown to be the case specifically around the time of the match, but later in the evening there's certainly a follow-on from people who have been at the match or have watched the match and have drunk all day. So it's often four to six hours afterwards that we would see the fall out from it. That is, as we would expect in the west of Scotland, people who have been drinking too much, and then disagreeing with their neighbours about who should have got a penalty and what the score should have been.'

Injuries, ranging from broken bones to bloody wounds, are part of the Old Firm day and inevitable, however well the match is policed. There tend to be few serious casualties around Celtic Park or Ibrox before, during and immediately after the games, and every football stadium has a team of medical staff on hand to treat any fans who are injured. Dr Sheridan is one of a number of medics, nurses, paramedics and first-aid staff who take their turn to work voluntarily at Celtic Park. On match days, three doctors, four ambulance crews and around forty first-aid staff at least are on duty, along with the Celtic club doctor and physio. They have access to a medical facility within the stadium and two ambulances, both with resuscitation equipment, that sit outside the ground in constant readiness to rush casualties to hospital.

On an Old Firm day, as the medical staff arrive around ninety minutes before the game kicks off, they notice more people congregating outside the ground, much more evidence of drunkenness among the supporters, and more singing, when normally fans walk to the ground quietly or talking among themselves. Inside, the stadium always fills to capacity, as nobody wants to miss an Old Firm game if they are lucky enough to have a ticket. The Rangers and Celtic supporters are too well segregated for any aggression to spill over into fighting, but the urgent press of a 60,000 crowd, the narrow aisles and rows between green plastic seats, the grey stone steps, the thick, green metal crash barriers, and the senses that have been dulled by alcohol, cause significant falls and impact injuries. Yet the passion for the game remains even once supporters have been seriously hurt, as though it is the final scoreline that is the greater concern.

'At the stadium, the vast majority of incidents are drink related at an Old Firm match,' Dr Sheridan says. 'The injuries are often from falling over. Colleagues who have been doing this for thirty, forty years tell me that it used to be a much bigger problem, before the licensing laws changed [no drinking has been allowed inside stadiums since the Old Firm riot at Hampden in 1980]. But people will go back to their seat with lacerations to their head, and occasionally with broken limbs, to watch the rest of the game, and then will go to hospital afterwards. I've seen somebody with a broken arm, and one with a broken ankle, who after receiving confirmation of their injuries, went back to their seat and were going to go to hospital afterwards because they wanted to watch the rest of the game. They feel the pain, but they want to make sure their team wins before they get treated.'

The match, in many ways, merely precipitates the trouble that occurs later in the day, often in and around pubs where it has been shown on television, or in residential streets when people have been drinking heavily while watching the game at someone's house, before then heading out. At Celtic Park, once the broken bones, cuts and bruises are attended to, the medical staff wait until they receive an instruction from the police and paramedic control rooms to stand down, often for as long as an hour after the final whistle, since the large crowd takes so long to disperse. The time can at least be passed with talk of the game, as there is little immunity to the influence of the Old Firm.

'Most of the people who work at the stadium will have an affiliation to one or the other,' says Dr Sheridan. 'Some of them are there just because they like being first-aiders, but the doctors, nurses and paramedics are there because they've an interest one way or another with the teams. It's the same in the hospital departments. Even people who have been injured, they will speak to the nurses, who are having a go at them for the state they've got into, about their team's result.'

It only takes a comment, or even just a certain look – disparaging, or scathing, of jubilation even – to spark a moment of brutality. The pub is busy, so that it requires gentle pushing and nudging just to reach the bar and place an order. The giant screen in the far corner is now showing Osasuna v. Real Madrid in La Liga, but few people are paying attention to the game. Earlier in the day, when the television had been showing Celtic v. Rangers, there had been little room to hold a pint without spilling it every time somebody jerked as they shouted at the screen, or muttered something spiky and abrasive under their breath, when the watching crowd of drinkers seemed taut and uncertain. A pile of empty glasses is stacked up at one end of the bar, waiting to be washed, but the staff are too busy as they work in a state of barely repressed frenzy, and the noise is chaotic.

A shard of angry voices suddenly slices through the chatter. The words are indistinct, but there is a tone of resentment. Bodies push frantically away from a space next to a table near the door. More shouts now, then a terrible, abrupt crunching sound. A woman screams, then a figure dashes out the door. When the crowd begins to separate, as if recoiling, a man can be seen lying on the floor, blood running down his face like thick rivulets of tears. His eyes look vacant, as if nothing has registered but shock. He puts his left hand to the side of his face, then looks with curiosity at his fingertips smeared in his own blood, as though they are somebody else's. On the floor, scattered a few feet away, lies a broken beer bottle. It has been used to stab him in the face. He wasn't wearing a team jersey, but the tassels of a football scarf can be seen poking out from the pocket of the jacket hanging on the back of his chair. 'The ambulance is coming,' somebody says, while people begin to return to their drinking.

Most paramedics hate working on the day of Old Firm games, because they are guaranteed to be busier than usual, and to be dealing with animosity and malice. In many cases, they will already have seen a life lost or someone hurt because they happened to support one football team rather than another, so they dread the consequences of the fixture. For all that the rivalry and the match is revered, it is capable of leaving a mournful legacy. Ever since the razor gangs of the 1960s, Glasgow's thugs have relied on knives or blades to assert themselves, and it is so prevalent that many disadvantaged teenagers – listless, disaffected, or already lost to a world of petty crime or drugs – carry them as a matter of course. Gang culture is present, but only in small, isolated pockets of the city, deprived areas where the prevailing attitude is of being abandoned by society, of being left to fend for yourself. The greater problem, on Old Firm days and in a more general societal sense, is the casual use of knives, so that an argument or a fight can quickly escalate into a serious assault. On a Friday and Saturday night, areas of Glasgow are awash with an insolent, almost defiant, drunkenness. The scene is no different from many other major UK cities, but the occasional outbursts of violence become savage and brutal when knives are involved.

There are different types of assault on an Old Firm day: the spontaneous slash or stabbing, often in the face; the wounds to the back, buttocks or legs, when the attackers are cold-eyed enough to target parts of the body that are unlikely to cause mortal injuries and so ensure that they won't face attempted murder charges if caught; and the particularly brutal injuries, when machetes or swords have been wielded and victims lose fingers, or are stabbed so deep that bones are exposed, or lungs are punctured. These assaults are so violent that it is often difficult to tell the difference between football bloodshed and serious criminal violence. Sometimes the weapons are just whatever comes to hand: a broken bottle or beer glass, or the sharpened edge of a gold sovereign ring. One nurse recalls a victim whose eyeball had been burst by a lead pipe, with viscous fluid sliding down the victim's face from the damaged eye socket.

At times, there is so much blood that the football jersey the victim is wearing is soaked in a dull, red colour and the club badge is obscured. On other occasions, the patient will not be wearing any colours, but it will be clear enough that the injuries are related to the Old Firm because they are talking about the game, or referring to it in their recollections of the incident. In the context of a 60,000 crowd, plus tens of thousands more who watch the game on television in the west of Scotland, the numbers of casualties and attacks are minor, yet they are significant in comparison to the normal admission rates in A&E departments in Glasgow and beyond. Football colours, blood, bandages, always the same combination.

At A&E wards, the staff are wary as the hours pass. There is a police presence, as it has been known in the past for patients on different sides of the Old Firm divide to clash with each other in hospitals, including conducting running battles and throwing chairs at each other. There is no formal advice on how to separate patients, and such skirmishes are less likely when the police are present, but the medical staff are trained to be vigilant and careful as they deal with the incoming victims and the patients' friends or family.

'Normally, by the time they get to the emergency department they've spent some time in the back of an ambulance or a police van, so they've calmed down,' says Dr Sheridan. 'But should there be rival fans in the department, that can flare things up again. It's not unusual for things to occur within the confines of the A&E department as well. But we have very good support from Strathclyde Police preventing these sorts of things, and the police presence in A&E departments on Old Firm weekends is pretty good. There's no definite segregation, but there is an unwritten decision-making process not to put people with different colours together, particularly when they're already inflamed by alcohol.'

Black humour is prevalent, and staff sometimes keep running scores of how many patients from each side of the divide have been treated in A&E department after an Old Firm game. It is a form of distraction, even if it must be difficult to remain calm when nurses wearing blue uniforms are referred to as 'fucking whores' by Celtic fans, and doctors in green scrubs are called 'Fenian bastards' by Rangers supporters. On the days of Old Firm games, assaults on hospital staff are also known to rise above the average.

Life-threatening injuries are rare, and most of the patients admitted are victims of common assault, often just dumped at the hospital door by friends who do not wish to become involved with the police. Some hospitals, like Monklands General – which lies between Airdrie, a predominantly Protestant area, and Coatbridge, which is historically mostly Catholic – have installed red cords outside the A&E department that these abandoned patients can pull to receive attention if they cannot make their own way inside.

'There is a real contrast when people do come in and start to calm down and receive treatment for their injuries,' Dr Sheridan says. 'They partake in lighthearted banter about the result and what's just happened, but one hour before, the red mist has come down and they've got involved in something they are now often regretting. Our department serves the north-east of Glasgow, and that has a number of socio-economic deprivation factors, and we certainly see that alcohol plays a significant part in people's attendances. It also seems to be affecting young people a lot more; we see a lot of young people with diseases that once we would only have seen in people in their forties and fifties. There are obviously still significant pockets of poverty in the city. It really depends on the importance of the match. The more important the match, the more agitated and upset people are, and the more they will drink and therefore the bigger the reaction will be afterwards.'

He is wearing a Celtic top, but claims he has no idea why he was attacked in the pub. 'Ah was out wi' ma girlfriend,' he says, slurring his words while his gaze drifts aimlessly across the floor. 'Ah dinnae know, do ah? I wis minding ma ain business, officer. Honest to God. I wiz oot wi' ma burd. Up the dancin'. Ah dinnae know.' There is a deep cut beneath his eye and a footprint on his back,

*where he was stamped on while lying on the ground. His breath,
thick and rasping, carries a stale smell of alcohol and cigarettes.*

*In the next cubicle, another man, with Rangers tattoos running
up both arms, including the club badge and a red hand of Ulster
symbol, is being treated for a minor stab wound to his thigh and a
slash across his back, which is superficial. He, too, refuses to elaborate
on who attacked him. He says he had just left his local social club
when two men walking past launched a brief assault. 'Shit happens,'
he mutters. A roll-up is tucked behind his right ear and the top of a
quarter bottle of Buckfast pokes out of the pocket of his jeans. 'I'll
take that, sir,' says the nurse when she enters. He looks at her suspi-
ciously, but hands the half-empty bottle over with a weary sigh. 'So
what happened then?' the nurse says. He looks back up at her. 'Nuthin.'*

Few victims press charges, or are even prepared to talk to the police
about how they sustained their injuries. In some cases, they simply
can't remember much about the incident; in others they are ashamed
to have been caught up in trouble and just want to put it behind them.
In certain circumstances, they will know their attacker and will either
seek revenge later, or want to avoid causing trouble in their own neighbourhood. Casualty staff become inured to the injuries, so that cases
are dealt with swiftly and moved on to other wards or discharged.

Professional detachment is a requirement of the job, but some
senior consultants and politicians have called for drastic action, such
as playing the game fewer times a season, or keeping a more detailed
record of admissions relating to the Old Firm encounters – often
difficult because the victims are so reluctant to speak formally to the
police – and then charging the clubs for the additional demand on
resources, in the manner of an insurance premium. There is also a
feeling that it is misleading to report after matches the number of

arrests made at the stadium, which has been falling steadily, but doesn't take into account the effect of violence on hospitals across the west of Scotland in the hours, and even days, after the game. Often, police figures will not refer to any incidents that occur two hours after a game as related to football. It was only after the Old Firm match that Rangers won 3–0 at Celtic Park in May 1999 to secure the title, when fights occurred outside the ground and well into the night, that changes to the scheduling of the fixture were made. Now, they kick off at lunchtime, and every effort is made to ensure that the result cannot be decisive in the Championship race.

'That match ten years ago had a significant impact on accident and emergency departments that day, there was a lot more people attending,' says Dr Sheridan. 'I was working when that Old Firm game occurred and the spill-on into the department that day was remarkable, and continued into the wee hours of the morning. Not only on the day of the match, but it often means that people will attend on the next day, the Monday, or even the Tuesday, where they've waited to present with their injury. Maybe they've woken up drunk with a broken hand, they've got a head injury, and it can be that they decided that they didn't want to attend A&E because they thought it would be too busy. The game altered a number of things, because of the spill-on and the amount of crime, disorder and A&E attendances. We've noticed that since the games have kicked off at lunchtime, there's less violence associated with that. People haven't had the chance to drink as much before, and if the game's finished by half past two, they will often go home initially before going back out again. There's only a hard core who will go out and drink all day. Now, even compared to a normal Saturday night or weekend, there's often an increase in attendances on the day of an Old Firm game, but because of the change to the time of the match and avoiding the title deciders, there has been an impact in reducing the number of attendances.'

It is also difficult to determine how many of the attacks are sectarian in nature; was somebody stabbed because they are a Celtic or Rangers fan, or because they are Catholic or Protestant? With the rivalry between the two clubs being split along religious lines, the distinction is often clouded, even if terms of abuse, such as 'Fenian' or 'Hun', are used. Nil By Mouth is a charity that was set up by Cara Henderson to campaign against sectarianism in 1999 after her school friend, Mark Scott, was stabbed to death while walking past a Rangers pub on his way home from a Celtic v. Partick Thistle game in 1995 while wearing a Celtic top. It works in classrooms, businesses and other settings, with volunteers telling of schoolchildren using sectarian terms without understanding what they mean. They are just repeating words they have heard in the home or the playground.

Sectarian attitudes remain embedded in the culture. Even if the days are over when certain industries or firms were widely known to favour Catholic or Protestant workers, and when Catholics could be sure that discrimination was still practised, abuse expressed in sectarian language is still prevalent within the Old Firm rivalry. Yet the game is not some kind of isolated expression of anger, recklessness or drunken aggression; hospitals across the country see a rise in A&E admissions following other tense football matches, such as derbies or established rivalries, like Aberdeen v. Rangers or Hearts v. Celtic, but mostly blunt traumas to the head and face rather than stabbings, which are a problem confined to Glasgow and its surrounding towns. Scotland, and the west central area in particular, is a country in which parts of society display a blithe attitude to alcohol and violence. Masculinity, conformity, a sense of belonging are all indelibly linked to drinking, which in itself is so prevalent that members of older generations, in particular, will often mutter: 'I dinnae trust anybody who's no a drinker, son. Never.'

What clutters up the ambulances and the hospital wards after an Old Firm game are the consequences of the rivalry between the two clubs. 'There's a general impression that due to health campaigns and the change in the smoking laws, and a number of other factors, that there is a slow improvement in Glasgow's health,' says Dr Sheridan. 'People's life expectancy in the vast majority of the city is increasing, and the facilities, sport or leisure, are improving, but there are certain areas where there has not been an improvement, despite active public health measures. In the last couple of years, [the level of violence relating to the Old Firm] has decreased, and in fact Glasgow's biggest attendances to A&E departments was after the Scotland v. France game [at Hampden in October 2006], when there was an inordinate amount of drinking, injuries and assaults afterwards, because of the importance of the match [it was a European Championship qualifying tie], the time that it occurred – on a Saturday afternoon, so people were drinking all day – and also because there were TV screens showing the match in Glasgow Green, so that large amounts of people then spilled into the streets of Glasgow on Saturday night and into Sunday. The Royal Infirmary had one of its biggest attendances ever after that match.'

The bell for last orders has been rung and the pub is beginning to thin out, reduced to a dwindling number of earnest, resolute drinkers. Two men sit near the window. A folded copy of the Racing Post lies on their table, with half the pages wrinkled after being doused in spilled beer earlier in the night. They are both contemplating the last dregs of their pints and their neat whiskies poured into small, short glasses, the thick golden liquid catching slivers of light.

'Ah fuck, we shoulda won that the day,' the larger of the two men says. His gaze does not lift from the two drinks sitting in front of him, but his friend nods in agreement. 'Aye,' he sighs. They are both unshaven and their eyes are translucent, as though

they can only see the world through a muddling gauze. 'Ah fuckin'
hate them,' the larger man says. 'They're scum, nuthin' but scum.
Ah hate them an' everythin' they fucking stand fir.' He lifts his
whisky glass from the table, his fingers wrapped around it so tightly
that the skin is pressed white against the surface, then drains the
contents in one go.

'What about that the day,' his friend says. 'Did you hear their
fans? Fuckin' trouble, that's all they know. Their songs and their
flags. Their fuckin' beliefs. Fuck them. And their team, dirty
bastards. Fuck them all.' He reaches for his pint glass, but then
changes his mind and downs his whisky in one curt gulp. 'Time
to go,' he says to his friend. 'Aye, fair enough. But we shoulda
fuckin' won that the day.'

Glasgow is a tribal city, and complex in the make up of its factions.
Football supporters are as likely to be middle class as working class,
and the attitudes to drinking and sectarianism differ across all groups,
so that generalisations cannot be made. Plenty of offensive and uninhibited behaviour is seen in the corporate seating areas of both Celtic
Park and Ibrox, as though wearing a suit somehow grants a dispen-
sation. This complexity, of allegiances and backgrounds and conduct,
is typical of a city that can sometimes feel as though it nurses a
fractured soul beneath its rough, hard exterior.

It is a place deeply influenced by its history, by the groups of people
who arrived in search of work during the great industrial revolution,
and shaped the place they found. Football so dominates the city
(because it was the working-class man's sport, something that reached
beyond the hardships of the Clyde dockyards and the narrow, grimy
tenements) that the two major clubs have become a means to express
the divisions that run through it. From Catholic and Protestant to rich

and poor, working class and middle class, to ignorant and educated. Each distinction collides with another, so that there is overlap among them, even when it comes to religion, as Scotland becomes increasing secular and faith turns, slowly, into a relic of previous generations. It is a divided community in many ways, uncomfortable with the nature of the divisions, but also fiercely defiant.

'Sectarianism in both Glasgow and Liverpool found expression in politics until the 1960s, yet its influence on football was very limited in Liverpool while marked in Glasgow,' says Graham Walker, Professor of Political History at Belfast's Queen's University. 'Perhaps it was the case that the Orange Order in Scotland widened its base beyond being a society for immigrant Irish Protestants much more than Liverpool. This widening of support was particularly notable in the years following World War I. The Rangers all-Protestant signing practice dates from WWI – there were several Catholic players before that. The Old Firm rivalry deepened in the inter-war years against the background of a socially troubled, economically deprived and culturally polarised society. Rangers acquired Protestant and Unionist associations at this juncture. Celtic had clearly been a club set up for and supported by the Catholic Irish immigrant community from its inception, and they were publicly identified with the Irish Nationalist cause. It has been suggested that pressure for Rangers to be all-Protestant came from the dressing room in the era of Bill Struth, but it was undoubtedly congenial to the boardroom, too. It was only in the 1960s that society's values and attitudes underwent the shift necessary to view the discrimination inherent in the club's (unwritten and unofficial) policy as damaging to Scotland's image. Then, just at this juncture, Northern Ireland erupted, echoes of its 'Troubles' were heard at Ibrox and Parkhead, and Scotland recoiled in fear of trouble spilling over as it did in the 1920s. There was in effect no public discussion of sectarianism for fear of exacerbating tensions in Scotland, and the political parties in Scotland avoided debate on Northern Ireland.

'In a sense, the working-class support base of the clubs presents a complication. Class consciousness and sectarian attitudes have seemed to co-exist. They arguably still do. Labour drew increasing support from the Protestant working class as well as (post-World War I) the Catholic community in the west of Scotland. For all the 'Queen and country' trappings around Rangers, there has always been a strong Labour political affiliation befitting the skilled workers character of the club's support for much of the twentieth century. For all the Celtic support's Irish Nationalist and Republican sympathies, they have been overwhelmingly Labour voters and thus supporters of a unionist party even if only a small "u".'

Rangers and Celtic, in the ways they were formed and have evolved, reflect this tangle of effects; they developed, at least in their size and their relevance, through sectarian division, rather than being the cause of it. After two decades of their existence, both clubs began to be marketed as the champions of the two sides of the ethnic divide, with Rangers being charged by the Protestant majority, and newspapers leader columns in particular, to counter the early success of Celtic. Once the second wave of Irish immigrants were drawn across to work at the Govan shipyards, the divide was deepened. There are plenty of supporters on both sides – perhaps even a growing majority – who abhor the sectarian singing, the references to Irish and Northern Irish history, the clinging on to aspects of their club's identity that they feel are no longer necessary. But the roots run so deep that they are almost impossible to wholly eradicate.

'I must confess that I think both clubs have done about as much as they can to shake off their past – or at least its worst elements,' says Bill Murray, an honorary research associate in history at La Trobe University in Australia and author of several books on the Old Firm and sectarianism in Scotland. 'But then again it is these "worst elements" that have made the Old Firm what it is. The more positive side is the way it has kept the crowds coming and the players staying in Scotland, although the latter is no longer the case. I must also confess that there is nothing quite like the atmosphere at these games. I have never heard such a degree of spontaneous hatred as I heard at Ibrox when an image of Billy Connolly [the comedian and a prominent Celtic supporter] appeared on the video screen before an Old Firm match.'

The two clubs continue to be defined by the past: Scotland being a predominantly Protestant country, the immigration of Irish Catholics and Protestants, the lingering legacy of the British Empire, all still resonate. It is an anecdotal, skewed history told in stories, half-truths and in the behaviour of parents, brothers and sisters, uncles, aunts, cousins and school friends. Where other west-coast British cities, such as Liverpool, Manchester, Birmingham and Cardiff, were shaped by similar influxes of people from Ireland, if they endured sectarian traumas, they happened much earlier than in Glasgow – Liverpool saw its worst riot between Protestants and Catholics in 1909 – and have moved beyond them by now. Similarly, in America, anti-Irish sentiment flared up then burned out in the 1850s and 1860s. The English cities also never witnessed the formation of a club so predominantly Irish Catholic as Celtic (or Hibernian in Edinburgh – or Dundee Harp). By 1912, there were indications that Rangers supporters were lining up behind the Unionist cause, while Celtic fans were associated with Nationalists, and these assumptions persist even now. In the 1920s and 1930s, militant political parties that were anti-Catholic were being formed in Glasgow, while in 1923 the Church of Scotland produced a report on 'The Menace of the Irish Race to our Scottish Nationality' (even in 1952, the General Assembly of the Church of Scotland was describing people from a Roman Catholic Irish background, whether they were first or second-generation immigrants, as 'a community largely of alien origin'); the social context was one of almost outright hostility.

Dundee, on the east coast, also received an influx of Irish immigrants, but the vast majority were Catholic, and this dynamic – the presence of very few Irish Protestants – is considered an explanation as to why this city has not suffered the same level of sectarian division as those on the west of the country. The first wave of immigrants from Ireland, around the 1850s, is believed to have been around two-thirds Catholic and one-third Protestant, and they brought with them a hostility to each other that was not evident among indigenous Scots.

'There does seem to be something distinctive about the Scottish situation,' says Professor Tom Devine, the Sir William Fraser Chair of Scottish History and Palaeography at Edinburgh University and the country's leading historian. 'First, the whole identity of Scotland up until the age of secularisation, probably starting around the 1960s, was Protestantism. The Reformation in Scotland was clearly a vital formative event in the nation's identity, but it was also in direct opposition to Catholicism. Also, in a sense, the deep-seated historical problems of the north of Ireland were decanted into Scotland and especially west central Scotland. Even to this day, you can pinpoint parts of Lanarkshire where there are settlements dating back to Ulster Protestant migration which have a continued reputation for Orangeism and also for substantial support for Rangers. These would include Harthill, Shotts, Larkhall, Airdrie, Newmains. That can be traced directly back to nineteenth-century Ulster immigrant settlement and I'm certain the majority of people today are completely unaware of this, but that is where their heritage comes from. The third factor is that unlike Liverpool, west central Scotland Irish, on both sides, maintained very strong connections, partly because of the ease of travel, with both societies in Ireland. That continues again to this day, because when there are Old Firm matches, the ferries are full.'

For many years, Scottish society, and particularly the Catholic Church and the Orange Order, were deeply concerned that the Troubles would also travel across the Irish Sea. It was evident in television and newspaper pictures that Unionist and Republican agitators in

Northern Ireland would often identify the allegiance to their cause by wearing a Rangers or a Celtic top. Many academics, politicians and church leaders believe that a form of sectarianism will remain in Scotland until there is a greater accord in Ireland about Ulster and its place in the country. Scotland, because of its history and the forces that shaped the Old Firm rivalry, is still sensitive to the impact of Irish Catholic and Protestant immigration.

'I don't think we'll see a settlement of the Irish problem in our lifetime,' says Devine. 'And I'm not convinced of the [argument that separate schools is a problem in Scotland], and I might say that, of course, given my background [in the Catholic faith]. But I'm thinking of it comparatively, and these institutions exist across the globe and don't seem to cause the same concerns of perceived effects as they do in Scotland. I do have a feeling that Catholic schools are being used as a scapegoat, and if you asked a member of the Catholic hierarchy – and this issue is very inchoate, very intangible – to suggest reasons why sectarianism is still alive in Scotland, particularly in west central Scotland, they would say because of the continuing unwillingness of mainstream Scottish opinion to accept Catholic schools, which are well known by any impartial research to be very good academically. That's why there's a particular, distinctive problem in Scotia. But the other thing to bear in mind is that we've passed through a revolution in terms of sectarianism. Labour market discrimination – what I call structural sectarianism – is at an end, although there are still people alive, mainly up in years, who both experienced it at the sharp end and who practised it. What remains is what I term attitudinal sectarianism. It could be regarded as bigotry. It's a strong feeling on the part of some influential figures in the Roman Catholic church that sectarianism is a fig leaf for anti-Catholicism.'

Bill Murray disagrees on the issue of separate schools in Scotland – where children are divided into Catholic and non-Catholic groups from age five onwards – believing that they play a significant role in forming attitudes that are later expressed in the Old Firm rivalry. The two clubs effectively represent sources of pride and identity for working-class communities, and so they have become dominant institutions in popular Scottish culture. Games between Rangers and Celtic then, perhaps inevitably, serve as opportunities to revert to a kind of behaviour and language that was once prevalent, particularly in a crowd dynamic, when individuals can lose their self-restraint because of the conduct of their peers.

'I used to agree with the safety-valve thesis, that to some extent it was better to get rid of some of this stuff in the regular bloodletting of Rangers against Celtic, rather than have it be demonstrated in some other way,' says Professor Devine. 'There was a view that it was an opportunity to let off sectarian steam. But the way I perceive it now is a bit different, because a lot of the old foundations of sectarianism – working-class Protestants voting for the Tories, Catholics voting for Labour, labour-market discrimination – are all gone. So you could argue, especially given the status of the two clubs, that because of their influence – and they can't be regarded simply as sporting institutions, they are major cultural institutions which affect people's identities – they have become, especially in the secular era, some of the main vehicles for this problem, in a way I wouldn't have thought they would have been in the 1950s and 1960s. They could be regarded as the last bastions. But it's because they're so hugely popular. There were more people down [in Manchester in May 2008 when Rangers played the Uefa Cup final and an estimated 150,000 to 200,000 supporters flooded into the city] than at the papal mass in Bellahouston [in September 2010]. It's astonishing the support that these clubs draw. Rangers don't have the same global reach as Celtic, because Celtic have in addition to the Scottish diaspora, the Irish diaspora. Rangers do have supporters' clubs across the globe, but they don't add up to that. Yet the Rangers support in Scotland is significantly bigger than that of Celtic.'

At a time when Scottish society has never been more integrated
– mixed marriages are at an all-time high, with sixty per cent of
baptised Catholics married to non-Catholics – many of the attitudes
expressed at an Old Firm game seem anachronistic; drawn out of
the clubs' past, but irrelevant to the contemporary culture. It is often
asserted that Rangers and Celtic, by their very presence, allow sectarianism to persist, and there might be some logic to the belief that
if the two clubs no longer existed, sectarian violence and rhetoric
would soon disappear from view. But the Old Firm are now deeply
established in Scottish life and much of the hostility that makes the
derby match so thrilling is traced back to their roots. What persists
is a residual hatred, which is the most difficult to eradicate, and
only continuing effective policing and education, by organisations
like Nil By Mouth and Sense Over Sectarianism, will gradually
diminish the more unacceptable aspects of the rivalry. But it will
always be a fierce, almost provocative confrontation, as the two clubs
will continue to influence the community identies of Glasgow and
the west of Scotland.

'Because of the horrors of de-industrialisation in the 1980s, we've
had the emergence, or a bigger expansion, of what's horribly referred
to as an underclass in Scotland,' says Devine. 'A lot of these people,
many of them without jobs, maybe even into a second generation,
achieve their identity, in so far as they've got any identity left, from
their support for these teams. That is something new. There were
long-term unemployed [in the past], people disabled through the
war, etc, but this culture which has developed in some parts of Scotland, and I would argue even more in the de-industrialised small
villages and towns of Scotland than in the big housing schemes in
Glasgow, there's more bitterness there. Through not fault of the
people, the economy's passed them by. This is a new element that
has attached itself to these to teams.'

The atmosphere of the Old Firm derby, with its its almost primal sense of confrontation, is intensified by a history that pre-dates even the game of football itself. The rivalry is unique because it formed in a city that was susceptible to religious and class division, so that Glasgow is now synonymous with football. When Celtic and Rangers meet, the game might even be said to be a Scottish derby, in the sense that they continue to represent the Catholic and Protestant communities, and because the country is too small to have allowed other teams to grow to a similar stature as the two Glasgow clubs (when Aberdeen and Dundee United won titles in the early 1980s, they still could not develop their fanbase significantly).

'I would observe that Celtic's well-heeled fans in professions like academia and the law have entered the debate around the Old Firm, determined to place it in the context of racism,' says Graham Walker. 'They have tried to apply the language and discourse of racism to it to serve the agenda of rendering it a "Rangers problem" or a problem of "Protestant Scotland". Sectarianism has been reinterpreted as anti-Irish racism, and the problem is viewed as rooted in Scottish history and society. This has brought a reaction from Rangers fans who point out that sectarianism is characteristic of many Celtic fans – of songs, chants about "Orange bastards" for example. They argue that if "Fenian" is taken to mean Catholic, then "Orange" is shorthand for Protestant. Ditto "Hun". They would also point to the way Celtic fans wave papal flags, wear "God Bless the Pope" scarves, as well as all the "Holy Goalie" stuff around Boruc. And these are the fans who complain about bringing religion into it. Rangers fans would also accuse the current Celtic support of fake Irishry, "Plastic Paddyism" which would be laughed at back in Ireland. Recently there has been the rise of the "Green Brigade", whose highly political display against the poppy commemorations grabbed headlines [in 2010]. This group has been responsible for banners depicting Ibrox on fire and slogans like "Let's Go to War" and "We don't care what the animals say". "Animals"? – imagine if that was Celtic fans so labelled. The Rangers fans' view is that Celtic fans' songs of hate are left unchallenged while every word of Rangers songs is scrutinised. And it is fair to say that the point about the songs is the spirit of hatred in which they are sung, rather than whether such and such a lyric is "offensive". The debate on sectarianism in Scotland of late has been notable by the attempts of one side to narrow it to one meaning – anti-Irish Catholic racism. This is to distort the reality. The debate has in effect been loaded by pressure groups and even by well-intentioned anti-sectarian campaigners.

'An example of what I mean by the debate being narrowed is the determination on the part of the "Celtic-minded" to rule out discussion of the schools issue. This subject has been central to the problem for nearly a century. There is a perception that in Scotland separate Catholic schools perpetuate a tribal identity which sustains its opposite and hinders the cause of social cohesion and interaction. The situation in Scotland is like Northern Ireland where there is a strong lobby for integrated education. In both places, Catholic schools make up the vast bulk of faith schools and are seen by some as receiving privileges as a result. In England and elsewhere, there are many different kinds of faith schools.

'The Irish question still informs the Old Firm controversy in Scotland. Recent dissident Republican activity has raised tensions. The fact that investigations recently involved taking suspects into custody in Dumbarton would have been enough to shape some people's opinions about being under threat or being unfairly vilified. Religious beliefs and practices may be in decline, but religious labels and identity still carry profound popular cultural significance and they continue to be influenced by events in Ireland.'

So when the supporters come to the game, they carry with them this immense history, a kind of obligation to stand defiantly for one side or the other, and for what those identities represent, even if they do not believe in every nuance themselves. There are other derbies

in cities across the world that are intense and raucous, and occasionally violent, but no rivalry can be considered quite so deeply forged
as the relationship between Rangers and Celtic. There is a pageantry
to the game, and it is the expression of the forces that enabled these
two clubs to become so significant in Glasgow, in Scotland, even
beyond. The noise, the colour, the naked aggression, it is the making
of Celtic and Rangers. 'There's no doubt that one week before an
Old Firm game there will be a sense of trepidation about what might
occur,' says Dr Michael Sheridan. 'That doesn't occur with any other
football match, or any other event in Glasgow.'

EPILOGUE

Another Old Firm game, the seventh of an inflamed, contentious season. At 12.30 p.m. on Sunday, 24 April 2011, Ibrox braced itself for the latest encounter between Rangers and Celtic. The stadium was filled by 50,248 supporters, and more police officers than had ever before controlled an Old Firm match. The rivalry was coming to a head, with Rangers leading by one point at the top of the Premier League table, but Celtic having one game extra to play. The two sides had met each other in all three domestic competitions – Celtic knocked Rangers out of the Scottish Cup after a replay, while the Ibrox side won the League Cup final at Hampden, and they had played three times already in the League – with every fixture becoming more ferocious. When volatile individuals like Scott Brown, the Celtic midfielder, and El-Hadj Diouf, the Rangers attacker, were added to the mix (the pair engaged in a running feud in one Old Firm game at Ibrox), the circumstances of each encounter became vulnerable to the kind of controversy that arose in the Scottish Cup replay at Celtic Park.

When the two teams met in the east end of Glasgow on the Wednesday night of 3 March 2011, the match ended with the home side winning 1–0, the referee Calum Murray showing more cards – including three reds, for Steven Whittaker, Madjid Bougherra and Diouf of Rangers – than any other official in more than two decades' worth of Old Firm games, and Ally McCoist, the Rangers assistant manager, making a comment to Neil Lennon, the Celtic manager, as they shook hands after the final whistle that caused Lennon to become so enraged that he had to be pulled away while snarling a furious response. These incidents were replayed on news and sport channels across the UK the following day, and Alex Salmond, the First Minister of Scotland, arranged a summit meeting between representatives of the two clubs, Scottish football's governing bodies and the emergency services. The police had previously raised concerns about the cost of dealing with Old Firm fixtures and of the upsurge of domestic violence incidents that occurred in the hours that follow each match, so that the trouble that flared in this game prompted a bout of national censure. With an election looming, the political response seemed driven by opportunism, and within football the feeling was of an over-reaction; Old Firm history is littered with more violent, more unruly incidents than those of this particular game, and where was the focus on Scotland's drink problem? If football was to be held accountable, why not also the nation's increasingly debilitating relationship with alcohol, which seems to be awash in the communities least prepared or able to cope?

Then four parcel bombs were intercepted in the mail system. Two were addressed to Lennon, one to Trish Godman, a Labour MSP known for her support of Celtic (she wore a team jersey to the Scottish Parliament on the day it broke up ahead of the 2011 election), and one to Paul McBride, a leading QC who has worked for Lennon and Celtic, while becoming an increasingly high-profile, if unofficial, spokesman for the club. And suddenly the football rivalry was reconstituted, into something darker, more malign. Earlier in the season, live bullets had been posted to Lennon and Niall McGinn and Paddy McCourt, two Northern Irish Catholics who play for Celtic, but all three chose to make little fuss. The parcel bombs – viable but crude, according to police sources – were a different order of threat, and they were traced to a postbox in Kilwinning, an Ayrshire town that is predominantly Protestant. The inference was that this act was sectarian – McBride is also Catholic, and although Godman is herself a Protestant, there was the subsequent discovery of a fifth parcel bomb addressed to Cairde na h'Éireann, a Republican organisation based in Glasgow – and part of a sustained campaign. A news blackout, enforced by the police while investigations were beginning (the parcel bombs were later thought not to be the work of a terrorist organisation), was lifted the week before the last Old Firm game of the season.

Celtic supporters rallied around Lennon, holding a candlelight vigil for him at Celtic Park one night and arranging a co-ordinated show of support for him in the final Old Firm game of the season at Ibrox, so that they came to consider him even more of a representation of their identity. Yet he is often portrayed as a divisive figure; many in the Catholic community believe that the hostility towards Lennon (he has been abused while driving, assaulted in the street several times and even found 'Neil Lennon RIP' painted onto the road outside his home) is caused by lingering sectarian attitudes that resurface in the presence of a brash, self-assured Northern Irish Catholic who is unabashed about his ambitions and who revels in his identity. Yet two of Lennon's predecessors – Tommy Burns, who was more open about his Catholic faith and more devout, and Martin O'Neill, a Northern Irish Catholic whose Celtic team initially swept Rangers aside and were dominant for much of his five years in Scotland – were not the victims of such violence and intimidation.

'It starts in the home,' Lennon said as he reflected on the hostility he has faced. 'It's passed down from generation to generation. You would like to think that in ten or fifteen years' time we won't have all this. But I'm ten years down the line and we're still talking about it. It's not a football issue, really. It's brought to the grounds, but it's nothing to do with what we deal with on a day-to-day basis. I don't know if there's a lot more that the clubs can really do about it.

Someone said that it's incurable – and it might just be that, in some instances. It's got to come from the home, first, more than anything to do with the schools or clubs. I was at the heart of it for five or six years; Martin O'Neill [former Celtic manager] made a point of [addressing] it. But that's six years ago and we're still talking about it. I'm not looking for any sympathy, though. I'm a football manager. Some of the things that get said to you at grounds are distasteful. I'm pretty much immune to it now. I'm not saying it's right, though; it's wrong. Unless people really take a heavy-handed approach to it, it's going to continue.'

There was an aggressive, hard edge to Lennon when he was a player (for Celtic, but also when he was at Leicester City), which made him a focus for the ire of opposition fans at many grounds beyond Ibrox. Some of that animosity remains, because it is only three years since he retired from playing, and he often rages in a similar way on the touchline as a manager. Many other individuals have been cast as Old Firm villains – Graham Roberts, the former Rangers defender, and Paolo di Canio, the Italian who played for Celtic, among them – but only Mo Johnston has ever been the target for sustained and credible threats to his life, after he signed for Rangers. The motivation for targeting Lennon, Godman, McBride and Cairde Na h'Éireann, whether the work of an individual or an organised group, cannot be known until a culprit is found guilty, but it can be little other than sectarian in nature. Lennon was surely targeted because he is a Northern Irish Catholic, and the threats revealed the bigotry that still exists in Scotland. Yet it was also perceived as a football issue, and so combined with other pressures on the Old Firm in what was a turbulent season.

'I played thirty-odd times for Northern Ireland while at Leicester and had no problems whatsoever,' Lennon said at the end of the season. 'As soon as I signed for Celtic and got picked again, that's when the problems began. We know the situation, there's the big

Catholic v. Protestant thing with Celtic and Rangers, but a lot of people just use that to hide behind to vent their sectarianism. I don't preach hatred to anybody, so it's hard to get your head round it. A lot of journalists would write that [Lennon brings it upon himself], but that's just an easy way of hiding behind it. I don't behave that differently from many other managers. When I played, it was because of my aggressive style, even although my disciplinary record was very good. So why does Niall McGinn and Paddy McCourt get it, and not other players?'

'I had to change a bit of my lifestyle obviously, and reassure my family that things are going to be okay,' Lennon said before the final Old Firm game of the season. 'My mum was a bit upset when I spoke to her. She was a bit drained, you know. My dad is there for her. He's a good crutch. It's just a question of reassuring her. But it leaves a bitter taste in my mouth. It's just another chapter in what has been a tumultuous ten years regarding things away from football. It's uncomfortable seeing yourself on the hour, every hour, on the news. It gets to the point where you are sitting in the hotel room on the day of the game and thinking, "Is that me they're talking about?" It's a surreal feeling. I have not had that since the death threat when I quit playing [for Northern Ireland] in 2002. So there is a disconcerting element to it. I had fourteen years in England with a completely peaceful, calm lifestyle. I could walk down the street without any hassle. It was a nice way to live your life. I never envisaged that coming [to Scotland] would create such hatred for myself or my persona as it has done. I don't know what it is that brings the worst out in people when it comes to myself. People have their theories. I was an aggressive footballer, blah blah blah, but they cannot have that theory now. It's obviously something else. And we all know what it is.'

In recent years, but this season especially, Celtic have been more assertive and confrontational, particularly in challenging the Scottish

Football Association. Although the club was not involved in the removal from office of Hugh Dallas, the head of refereeing, after he forwarded an email containing a joke about the pope, and Dougie McDonald, Scotland's leading referee, after he lied to Lennon about how he changed the award of a penalty at Tannadice in October 2011, the perception was that Celtic were supportive of these decisions. Implicitly, in letters sent to the SFA requesting clarification about certain refereeing decisions, the club has also raised the notion of officials being biased against Celtic – a sense of persecution that the club's supporters have held for many years. There has never been any evidence of officials setting out to treat the club unfairly, and even McBride, a former grade-one assistant referee, says that he never encountered any such organised prejudice. Yet evident in the challenging of the SFA's authority, and the use of the high-profile McBride as the club's legal representative in appealing a six-match touchline ban against Lennon, was a more strong-willed, self-confident Celtic, one emphasising a kind of siege mentality: them against us.

This is clear, too, in the increasing focus on the club's Irish heritage, which is partly emotional and partly economic (the large Irish diaspora that is readily prepared to see Celtic as emblematic of their background and culture is a resource the club can tap into). Older generations of supporters do not recall this Irish identity being so prominent – Irish folk tunes are played before games and the club magazine urged supporters to register their Irish roots in the 2011 census – but then this might also be typical of emigrant communities. The first generation, particularly if they feel persecuted, seek only to survive, and so congregate among numbers of their own kind. The next generation look to assimilate themselves, to fit into their surroundings; third and fourth generations, having become seamlessly integrated, then look back to their roots to gain an understanding of themselves and their heritage, and then feel confident in recognising it. Celtic have become so identified with their

Irish Catholic background that Republic of Ireland strips and Irish tricolours are prominent among the support, although much of that can also be interpreted as a provocation to Rangers supporters.

At the same time, many Rangers supporters have had to come to terms with the loss of some old certainties. There was a time when working-class Protestants could enter a trade and be sure that they were in a job for life. At the same time, the Church of Scotland was a strong presence in their lives, and a deep sense of entitlement was passed down the generations. Now, the nature of Scotland's industries is changing and support for independence from the United Kingdom is growing. As the songs they once sung with impunity are finally being banned, they feel under siege, as if their identity is slipping away. Where Celtic fans celebrate their heritage, Rangers supporters feel that theirs is being assailed.

There is an eternal struggle between the two clubs: every action cannot be seen in isolation but in the way it affects, or is addressed to, the other side. Celtic fans celebrate (rightly) their club's inclusiveness and the fact that so many of their great figures – such as Danny McGrain, Kenny Dalglish, Jock Stein – were Protestant and grew up supporting Rangers, whereas for so many years the Ibrox club tried to avoid signing Catholics. In the same way that Celtic's Irish roots are more conspicuous, Rangers fans have become more Unionist, with more Union Jack flags seen at games than there would have been in the middle decades of the last century, and 'Rule Britannia' and 'God Save the Queen' often sung at games. Rangers' only significant historical connection to Northern Ireland comes from the Protestant emigrants who travelled across the Irish Sea to work at the Harland and Wolff shipyards in Govan, bringing their enthusiasm for the Orange Order and a renewed anti-Catholic bias with them, yet Northern Ireland flags and strips are prevalent at Ibrox. It can seem as if so much of the identity of these two Scottish clubs has been appropriated, but then there seems little willingness at boardroom level to eradicate these associations when they strengthen and spread the reach of the clubs' fanbases. Rangers, too, are aware of the commercial worth of the club becoming symbolically pro-Union, while supporters glorify in the description of the club being 'quintessentially British'. The team also often travels to Belfast to play friendlies against Linfield at Windsor Park, the national stadium of Northern Ireland, where there is a strong support for the Ibrox side, and for many of the values that have become associated with the Rangers support.

The two clubs are involved in anti-sectarian initiatives, but a minority of supporters on both sides of the divide continue to be a problem. Among Celtic fans, pro-IRA songs can still be heard, along with references to Huns and Orange bastards, offensive terms that seek to demonise Protestantism. Rangers supporters call upon a greater variety of sectarian chants, or 'Fenian' add-ons to songs, and it can seem at times as if they express their identity solely as a form of anti-Catholicism; whereas Celtic fans can sing Republican folk songs that romanticise a political struggle for independence, Rangers seem bound to respond, and so define themselves, in opposition to this. The reality is more complex, but in 2011 both sets of supporters feel persecuted: Celtic fans for perceived injustices against them and their manager, but also the notion that they are as guilty as their rivals – there is a general refusal to acknowledge offence caused by IRA or 'Hun' songs, or at least to bracket them in the same way as The Famine Song, a chant described by an appeal court judge as racist – and Rangers supporters for being punished by Uefa for sectarian songs heard at Europa League matches: 'No Pope of Rome' (which includes the lines: No chapel to stand in my eye / No nuns and no priests / Fuck your rosary beads / Every day is the 12th of July) and 'The Billy Boys' returned this season having previously fallen out of use.

'When I was a Rangers supporter it was fifty years ago. I started going in my early teens and when I sang the songs I had no realisation of what they meant, but I sang them,' says Walter Smith. 'That was regarded as part of the traditions but it didn't mean anything to me at the time and it doesn't mean anything to me now. It's still an aspect a lot of supporters look upon as a traditional aspect of the club, but it's no longer acceptable therefore they shouldn't do it. For me, such singing cannot be a part of the club in the modern era. I think I have given out that message before, and I think the club has given out that message before. My own message again is, the singing has to stop. It's like everything else: what was acceptable twenty or thirty years ago is not acceptable any longer. But you are also talking about a situation that has for a long time been part and parcel of the club, and was never frowned upon in the manner that it is today. There is no doubt there has to be a change.'

This has been a critical time at Ibrox, with the club up for sale while carrying a heavy debt to Lloyds Bank that saw the squad reduced and Smith unable to sign a player on a permanent contract for two seasons. Rangers fans felt besieged, at the same time as Celtic were becoming more self-possessed; then Lennon took over as manager and even the Ibrox side's dominance on the pitch – two consecutive league titles under Smith – was threatened.

The nature of the rivalry between the two clubs does not change, but it remains susceptible to fluctuations caused by cultural and sociological influences. At a time when church and chapel attendances are falling, and thirteen years on from the signing of the Good Friday Agreement in Northern Ireland, the two sets of Old Firm supporters seem more assertive about their (religious) identities than they have been for many years. And all of these factors: the condemnation, the songs of the supporters (in particular the Rangers fans, under scrutiny by Uefa) and the tightness of the Championship race shaped a season in which the Old Firm relationship seemed more hostile.

'Times are good in Northern Ireland now. Belfast is one of the nicest cities in Europe, everyone is visiting it now, it's fantastic. But people here use football as a vehicle to deliver hatred,' said Kenny Shiels, the Kilmarnock manager who comes from Northern Ireland and whose brother was murdered during the Troubles, speaking as the season drew to a close. 'What are they going to do in the summer when football isn't there, in Glasgow or Edinburgh? I don't think sectarianism is prevalent in society here, it's just been taken into football and they use it because there's big crowds and lots of people watch the games. It's not there in Northern Ireland, which is good, even though there's isolated incidents. I don't see how it all adds up here. A lot of these people have never been to their roots, the ones going to the games. On one side, they sing about the Boyne and places like this – they don't even know where it is. The sash my father wore? My God, they haven't got a clue. They just use it as a social vehicle, after a few drinks. It's about insecurity and creating a bond between other fans. The good supersedes the bad. But when it's bad, it explodes out of all proportion. It was a disgrace what happened to Neil [Lennon]. I don't know how it's allowed to come into football, it shouldn't. I think it's Neil's profile. There's now an element of hatred towards him in Scotland. It's a sensitive subject but people have this identity and, for some reason, there's a poisonous hatred towards him. If it wasn't happening to Neil, we probably wouldn't talk about it – because it doesn't deserve the coverage. People keep saying it's about his personality but all he's trying to do is manage a football team. He should be commended for that, for having a passion for his team and defending the club. He speaks well of his players and that's what managers are there to do.'

The threats to Lennon were of a different nature; something beyond the football rivalry. During his playing days he was twice attacked in the street, and on one occasion needed hospital treatment. He has required 24-hour protection and a Hearts supporter even jumped onto the touchline at Tynecastle and charged him (which prompted a vicious response from the Celtic fans, who attacked stewards and fiercely chanted about the Provisional IRA). While Lennon generates an antagonism in a football context – something widespread beyond the Old Firm rivalry and which is something that has always inspired in him a defiant response – the bullets and the bombs were sectarian threats that revealed Scotland's ongoing problem with old tensions and hatred. Lennon and the others were targeted because of their religion and their affiliation to Celtic, a reality that many in Scotland seem uncomfortable accepting. Using Lennon's occasionally aggressive nature as a form of explanation for this intimidation is absurd, and an evasion of the real issue: that areas of Scotland still harbour deep-seated anti-Catholic resentment. The Old Firm have grown and thrived because of the two sides of the religious divide that they represent, but the consequence is that they are also isolated and exposed by it. Victimhood doesn't rest easily on so forthright and resolute a figure as Lennon, and he has coped admirably with a level of abuse that has been sustained and hateful. He has galvanised the Celtic support, and Ally McCoist might do the same for Rangers as he succeeds Walter Smith as manager, but the season has been traumatic and discouraging.

'It's just not right,' said Walter Smith ahead of the final Old Firm game of the season, and after he and the Rangers coaching staff were told to be alert for suspicious parcels in the post. 'It's only a football match, for goodness sake, nothing else. You've got to condemn what has happened out of hand. To be honest, I'm glad to be getting out of it. We've been surrounded by it for all these years. It's been highlighted recently, with all the sectarian singing, but the sectarianism separating the two clubs has always just been part and parcel of what the two clubs were, in a situation which is just life in the west of Scotland. We have handled that aspect, maybe to our detriment, by ignoring the majority of it and just getting on with it. But when we have reached the stage, as we have now, when it goes further than that with threats to people's lives, then I question whether it is all worthwhile. It's just a football match, after all, between two great clubs. But it is degenerating into something far worse than just the sectarian aspect, or sectarian singing. It is just totally unacceptable.

'We've got to say that [the fault] rests with society and the way life has been led in the west of Scotland for a great number of years. What we are talking about here isn't just the traditional aspects of sectarian singing and chanting which go on during a game, or calling one manager one thing or another. This is taking it into a far more serious realm that I can ever remember. It's always been there and we just carried on with it, because it was part and parcel of our lives where we were brought up. Because you have to say that in the west of Scotland, the football is the aspect that brings up the sectarian issue on a regular basis. The situation surrounding it just now is such a pity, because Rangers and Celtic are two great traditional football clubs. We should be concentrating on that. I feel Scotland is fortunate to have them. If you have two great clubs in one city, you are going to have a great rivalry.'

All of these factors were carried into the final Old Firm game of the 2010/11 season, and combined with the taut competition at the top of the Premier League. The increased numbers of police officers were instructed by their superiors beforehand to act on any sectarian singing, which the supporters were warned about in the run-up to the game. It felt like a pivotal moment, something that rose above the outcome of a football match.

Before kick-off, as 'Penny Arcade' was played over the Tannoy system, Ibrox became a cradle of noise. Small Union Jack flags had been left on the seats of the home supporters, and they fluttered as they were waved enthusiastically in the midday air, while tricolours were raised among the away support. The clamour was urgent, irresistible, heartfelt and relentless. In the eighteenth minute of the game – a time chosen because Lennon wore the No. 18 shirt as a Celtic player – the away fans stood to applaud and chant the manager's name. The Rangers fans responded by raising their own noise, then three sides of the stadium became a heaving mass of people as they bounced up and down. For a few moments, the football being played was irrelevant; instead, two sets of supporters, without rancour, tried to outdo each other in their support for their side, for their cause. It was invigorating, stirring, dramatic; a spontaneous outpouring, and it contained no sectarian or offensive chanting. Sitting within it, you could feel both hopeful, for a future that might see the intolerance of the Old Firm relationship diminished, and sad that this might only be a brief glimpse, that the antipathy, expressed in hateful language against Fenians and Huns, would endure.

INDEX